GW00357304

MY NAME IS MICHAEL CAINE

MY NAME IS MICHAEL CAINE

Anne Billson

With photographs from the Kobal Collection

MULLER

London Sydney Auckland Johannesburg

By the same author

Screen Lovers

I would like to express my gratitude to the following people for their help: Mike Hodges, Chris Peachment, Christopher Petit, Kim Newman, David Thompson, and the staff at the BFI library.

Anne Billson

This edition first published in 1991 by Muller

Random Century Group Ltd
20 Vauxhall Bridge Road, London SW1V 2SA

Random Century Australia (Pty) Ltd
20 Alfred Street, Milsons Point, Sydney, NSW 2061, Australia

Random Century New Zealand Ltd
PO Box 40-086, Glenfield, Auckland 10, New Zealand

Random Century South Africa (Pty) Ltd
PO Box 337, Bergvlei, 2012, South Africa

BRITISH LIBRARY CATALOGUING-IN-PUBLICATION DATA

Billson, Anne
My name is Michael Caine: A life in film.
I. Title
791.43092

ISBN 0-09-175055-5 (hardback)
ISBN 0-09-175336-8 (paperback)

Set in Baskerville by SX Composing Ltd, Rayleigh, Essex
Printed and bound in Great Britain by
Butler & Tanner Ltd, Frome and London

CONTENTS

INTRODUCTION

This is not a biography of Michael Caine. It is an attempt to demonstrate – with the help of selected biographical details, reviews of his performances, and more general film criticism which will place those performances in context – that Michael Caine is the best, most important, and most versatile film star that Britain has ever produced.

Let us consider the competition. Cary Grant may have been born in Britain, but his claim to fame is as the greatest actor in American cinema, and he must be designated an honorary American. Laurence Olivier is often hailed as the best and most important British stage actor of the Twentieth Century, but his screen performances are of variable quality. Robert Donat, David Niven, Leslie Howard are wonderful Englishmen, but Hollywood Englishmen. Stewart Granger is dashing in costume, less comfortable in modern clothes. John Mills has a fine stiff upper lip, but tends to overdo it in character roles. Michael Redgrave never lived up to his promising start. James Mason is a mesmerising screen presence who never quite made it into the top ranks. Jack Hawkins and Trevor Howard can be splendid but lack sex appeal. Rex Harrison, Ralph Richardson, John Gielgud are lovable but limited; Alec Guinness is too much the chameleon. Robert Shaw never realised his potential. Richard Burton gave too many hammy performances. Peter Sellers went downhill in the Sixties. Alan Bates tailed off in the Seventies. Richard Harris, Peter O'Toole and Albert Finney all had hiccups in their careers. Terence Stamp took time off to meditate. Roger Moore is Roger Moore.

As for contenders from the female camp, audience expectations and social conditioning have ensured that no British film actress can even come close. Britain has never produced a Garbo or a Dietrich, Davis or Crawford. Besides, photogenic beauty has always been more highly prized than versatility in an actress, and the lack of roles for middle-aged women has sent many a career into premature decline. Madeleine Carroll, Vivien Leigh, Deborah Kerr and Jean Simmons all had bright moments, but their stints in the first division were relatively brief. Vanessa Redgrave, Glenda

The breakthrough role; Lieutenant Gonville Bromhead in **Zulu.**

Jackson and Maggie Smith have been sidetracked by political or theatrical concerns. The women are non-starters here.

Caine's only possible rival is Sean Connery. It is no coincidence that each actor has a distinctive voice which neither has to modify for the American market; it is the sign of a major star that the roles are tailored to fit the accent, instead of the other way round. How can audiences learn to love Meryl Streep if she is always trying on other people's voices? Robert Redford spoke like Robert Redford in *Out of Africa*, even though he was supposed to be playing an Englishman, whereas Bob Hoskins, a Londoner like Caine, and bordering on international appeal, has always adopted an American accent in his Hollywood films.

Connery's sex appeal is more obvious than Caine's, but he is cast from a more orthodox heroic mould. One could see him replacing Caine in the Frederick Forsyth thriller *The Fourth Protocol* or even clowning opposite Steve Martin in *Dirty Rotten Scoundrels,* but it is much harder to imagine him taking over from Caine in *Dressed to Kill, Deathtrap* or *Hannah and Her Sisters.* Connery can deliver a quip with the best of them, but his grasp of light comedy is not as sure as Caine's. And while Caine has been known to play characters with no redeeming features whatsoever, Connery never plays villains, hardly ever plays losers – and on those rare occasions when he does play them, you can be sure they are *noble* losers. So though he might challenge Caine for the title of Best and Most Important, in the Most Versatile stakes it is no contest.

Of Britain's three internationally-known movie-stars, Caine is the only one who has never played James Bond. While Caine as 007 might seem rather a far-fetched notion nowadays, it is an interesting exercise to consider how he might have approached the role if by some quirk of fate it had been pushed in his direction, back in the days before his image had been locked into place by *The Ipcress File* and *Alfie.* Caine as Bond: one of the most outrageous what-ifs of our time, and yet he could have done it, no question. The London accent would have had to go, but the hooded eyelids and the banked-up menace which would later emerge in *Get Carter* and *Mona Lisa* would have been given free rein. His 007 would have turned out wholly different from Connery's, less of a bounding action man, perhaps, and more of a deadly fop, not a million miles from the anti-hero of *Get Carter.* But then Connery's Bond – superb though he was – was not exactly what Ian Fleming had had in mind when he had created the character. In the end, it was Caine who provided the alternative to Bond – down-to-earth Harry Palmer in *The Ipcress File,* the sort of secret agent who would buy his clothes off the peg and who, after a fight, might put in an expenses claim for dry-cleaning.

It is over twenty-five years since Michael Caine first appeared in a leading role in a movie. Since then, he has worked non-stop, appearing in spy thrillers, costume dramas, romantic comedies, psycho-thrillers, horror films, disaster movies, action adventures, caper movies, slapstick comedies, war pictures . . . About the only kind of film he's never appeared in is a Western.

He has travelled around the world to strange and exotic places, from the Caribbean to the Far East, from Finland to Brazil – and foreign food can still give him stomach upsets. He lives the life of a movie-star, but is completely lacking in vanity. He enjoys his money, and he also gives generously to good causes. Caine lives the comfortable, movie-star life with a glamorous wife, the sort of life he can only have dreamed about as a child. And yet he has achieved that dream on his own terms, and with a minimum of creative torment. He has studied the art and craft of screen acting for more than three decades, and he is generous in passing his accumulated knowledge on to younger actors. He knows that if you are caught 'acting' in a movie you are doing it wrong. He works hard, makes it all look easy – and still there is that indefinable something, the X factor, the secret ingredient which the movie camera can't help loving.

He is the best, most important, and most versatile film-star that Britain has ever produced.

'To be a movie star, you have to invent yourself.'

Michael Caine invented himself in textbook fashion. Years later, in fact, he would produce the very textbook – *Acting in Film,* a transcript of the BBC master class he taught in 1987. 'I was a Cockney boy and obviously didn't fit anybody's idea of what an actor was supposed to be, so I decided to put together elements that added up to a memorable package.'

If your definition of Cockney is strictly someone from a specific area of London's East End, then this is all part of the invention as well. Maurice Micklewhite was born on 14 March 1933 in St Olave's Hospital, Rotherhithe – a bit of a hike from Bow Bells, and a bit of a swim over the Thames as well – and was brought up south of the river, on the edge of that terrifying Tube-free void where the good folk from North London throw up their hands and get hopelessly lost. Maurice grew up in the same part of London as Charlie Chaplin, and you don't often see Chaplin called a Cockney: then again, Chaplin made films in which he never had to open his mouth. But Cockney is a useful identity for a would-be star to latch on to; tell an American you're from Kennington, or Walworth, or Camberwell, and he'll probably look blank. But tell him you're a Cockney, and he'll instantly know where you're coming from.

Maurice's father, also called Maurice, was one of the 'irreducible million', men who were continually unemployed between the wars, though in 1936 – the year Maurice's brother Stanley was born – the 'irreducible million' was reduced by one when he found a job as a porter in Billingsgate fish market. Whenever the cash ran low, his wife, Ellen, would take on odd jobs cleaning or sewing on buttons. But Mr Micklewhite preferred her not to work; in the blue collar scheme of things, a woman's place was in the home, while the men went down the pub. It was a background tough enough to make Maurice want to escape from it, but it seems to have been secure in every aspect apart from the financial. Times were hard, but Ellen Micklewhite made sure her family never went cold or hungry. Later, she supported Maurice through thick and thin, standing by him all the way through his years of hardship. She sounds like a mum in a million.

For the first six months of his life, Maurice lived with his parents in a slum on the Old Kent Road until they had to leave because it was being knocked down. The family moved a short way south-west, to a two-roomed flat just off the Camberwell Road. The building housed three families and there was one toilet to be shared by all twelve occupants.

Michael Caine would later say, 'Every place I ever lived in as a kid has been demolished. Sometimes I feel that my past has been demolished.' One is tempted to conclude from this that he feels Maurice Micklewhite has also been demolished. But Maurice is still in there. You can see signs of him peeping out in interviews through the years, especially when Caine discusses his nest-building activities. Perhaps to compensate for all that overcrowding and toilet sharing, Caine has always attached a great deal of importance to his home, whether a trendy pad shared with Terence Stamp at the height of swinging London or a bachelor flat in Grosvenor Square, an old mill in Berkshire, a house high in Beverly Hills, or a converted rectory in Oxfordshire. He has been more than usually willing to open his doors to visiting journalists, happy to outline his plans for conversions and extensions, enthusiastic in his praise of gardening as the ultimate therapy. Through the years, the scale of the nest-building expanded until, in the mid-Eighties, nearby villagers complained about the noise and volume of heavy traffic

Maurice Micklewhite takes a look at his Bermondsey roots.

when he was adding a conservatory, lake and whirlpool bath to his new Oxfordshire home.

During the Second World War, Maurice had a taste of life very different from the one he knew in South London. While Mr Micklewhite went off with the British expeditionary force, the rest of the family was evacuated to a village in Norfolk where they lived for the next six years. For some of this time, Mrs Micklewhite worked as a live-in cook for a local timber merchant. It was in this house that Maurice Micklewhite first encountered sandwiches with the crusts cut off.

After the war the Micklewhites were rehoused in a prefab near the Elephant and Castle; their previous home had been flattened in the Blitz. Maurice, who had passed his scholarship exam in Norfolk, was attending a grammar school in Camberwell, but felt out of place there. He acquired his first pair of spectacles and spent a lot of time reading in Southwark Public Library. And he went to the cinema six or seven times a week, usually through skiving off games lessons. He came from a tough neighbourhood so his heroes, naturally, were the tough guys: Humphrey Bogart, Errol Flynn, John Wayne – especially Bogart, who he later declared was his favourite actor of all time. Already, Maurice Micklewhite was bitten by the star bug; already he had made up his mind he was going to be a rich and famous movie actor. From the age of eleven onwards, he was watching to see how it was done. He watched Spencer Tracy, for instance. 'He was so good you couldn't tell when he was acting and when he wasn't.'

It is worth noting that Caine's heroes were all American. British stars, by contrast, tended to be theatre-trained RADA graduates with upper-crust accents. Cockneys signalled comic relief or a bit of low-life colour, and Maurice noticed their accents were never right. Maurice Micklewhite just wasn't the *type* to become an actor; there was no precedent, as they say in court. But not far from where the Micklewhites lived was Clubland, a youth club with a drama group attached. In 1947 Maurice ended up in the drama class, apparently in pursuit of a girl he fancied, though this might well have been a convenient way of taking up the acting lark without being thought a cissy by his friends. He appeared in a couple of productions, including a translation of Karel Čapek's *R.U.R.* in which he played a robot, and the group chairman was soon referring to him in his reports as 'the best actor in the club'.

At around this time, Maurice borrowed a translation of Vsevolod Pudovkin's book, *Film Acting,* from the library. Shortly after the First World War, Pudovkin (whose most famous film was *Mother,* made in 1926), had studied technique at the Soviet State Film School under Lev Kuleshov, and had been impressed by Kuleshov's experiment in which the face of an actor was intercut with footage of a bowl of soup, a child and a coffin. To onlookers, the actor appeared to be expressing emotions appropriate to each object, whereas in fact his facial expression had not altered at all. From this and other similar exercises, the Russians concluded that the trick was all in the editing. The conclusion to be drawn was that, for an actor on film, less means more; give audiences an expressionless face and they will read into it whatever they need to see. From Pudovkin's book, Maurice learned two things: film acting was not acting but re-acting, and film actors should try not to blink. 'Blinking makes your character seem weak,' Caine would tell his master class many years later. 'Remember: on film that eye can be eight feet across.'

In 1950, Maurice left school with his School Certificate diploma and squeezed in some experience as a filing clerk and messenger boy for film companies in Victoria Street and Wardour Street. Thirty years later, a producer dug out a snap of him and sent it to *Screen International*; the producer remembers him as tall and gangling, willing and hardworking – someone who obviously loved being in the film business. He was also taken on as teaboy during the shooting of *Morning Departure,* a stiff upper lip submarine movie starring John Mills and Richard Attenborough.

This brief flirtation with the film world came to an end, however, in 1951, when his call-up papers summoned him to do two years' National Service. He spent the first year in Germany as a private in the Queen's Royal Regiment, and the second year with the Royal Fusiliers, on active service as part of the United Nations force providing support for South Korea against the Communists in the North. He hated the army, with its petty restrictions and rigid class structure. Active service, he soon found out, was hours of boredom punctuated by a few terrifying seconds of lethal gunfire. He was offered a promotion to Lance-Corporal, but decided to stay a Private. 'I was always very aware that I was a pawn who didn't matter very much.'

Caine used his experience in the army in his very first starring role, in *Zulu*; he based his performance of Lieutenant Gonville Bromhead, in part, on one of his platoon commanders. Later, on location for *Play Dirty,* he would remember what it was like to be under fire for real. 'You were talking to somebody, and a minute later he wasn't there.'

His first-hand experience of combat was to stand him in good stead in other ways, as well. 'It was in Korea that I noticed heroes weren't all six feet three, with perfectly capped teeth, but ordinary guys,' he said. 'So that's the way I try to play them.'

1

THE GALLEYS

After emerging unscathed from his stint in Korea, Maurice Micklewhite found a job in Smithfield market, churning large amounts of butter. One day he confided his acting ambitions to a foreman, who borrowed a copy of *The Stage* from his daughter, an aspiring singer, and brought it into work. Micklewhite found an advertisement for an Assistant Stage Manager for Horsham Repertory Company, a position which also offered occasional walk-on parts. He applied and got the job, which turned out to be that of general dogsbody, running errands, painting and decorating, moving scenery, sweeping the stage and clearing up after performances. After two weeks, he took on his first professional role, that of a policeman who marched on stage at the play's end, grabbed the villain's arm and said, 'Come along with me, sir.' After that, he played a butler with the line, 'Dinner is served,' and a more substantial butler role came his way when it turned out he was the only member of the company capable of speaking with a credible Cockney accent. 'I grew up in British rep,' Caine said many years later, 'playing old characters with flour in my hair. I liked the variety.'

It was around this time that he stopped being Maurice Micklewhite. The name Maurice didn't have that leading-man ring about it; the only well-known Maurices in the business were the excellent British character actor Maurice Denham and the French entertainer Maurice Chevalier. The manager of Horsham Rep decided something a little catchier was required. Everyone had been calling him Mick anyway, because of his surname, so he settled for Michael, Michael Scott. The name Scott was a popular stage-and-screen-name for actors; Randolph Crane had adopted it and gone on to become one of the best-loved actors in Westerns, while Emma Matzo, who had once understudied Tallulah Bankhead on Broadway, was now better known to audiences as Lizabeth Scott. In 1947, she had played opposite Bogart in *Dead Reckoning*; Caine would one day work with her on *Pulp*.

After nine months at Horsham, Michael Scott was laid low by a bout of cerebral malaria, a souvenir of his service in Korea. Hospitalised in Roehampton, he was dosed with pills and emerged after seven weeks minus four stone in weight. Armed with another copy of *The Stage,* he applied and was accepted for a job in repertory at the Lowestoft Theatre, Suffolk. Here he met Patricia Haines, an actress from Sheffield, who would shortly become his first wife. She later said that the first thing she noticed about him was his long, golden eyelashes – the heavy-lidded *Alfie* look in embryo, perhaps, though she didn't say whether his gaze was unblinking.

The relationship was not an easy one. On stage, Michael Scott had to play second fiddle to his leading lady, though he was gradually being cast in bigger roles. At home, their frequent arguments were exacerbated by lack of money. When the repertory season came to an end, they were forced to stay with Michael's parents in the Elephant and Castle prefab. When they found somewhere to live, it was a two-roomed flat in Brixton, with no hot water. This was not the recipe for a happy marriage.

Michael began to land bit-parts in TV plays and series, but Equity informed him they already had a Michael Scott on their books; he would have to change his name again. In August 1954, he went to see Bogart playing the paranoid Captain Queeg in *The Caine Mutiny,* showing at the Odeon Leicester Square. Afterwards, still mulling over the name change, he caught sight of the film's title on display outside the cinema. *Caine.* It looked good in lights, he thought, and so *Michael Caine* it was.

He couldn't have settled on a better handle. He might not have considered it at the time, but the name would turn out to be a headline-writer's dream. Over the next thirty-five years, journalists would go to town with variations on CAINE MUTINY, CAINE SCRUTINY, CAINE IS ABLE, CITIZEN CAINE, DRY CAINE and even CAINE TOAD. *Micklewhite* didn't offer the same opportunities, *Scott* just didn't have the same pizzazz and besides, it was too popular. *Halliwell's Filmgoer's Companion* lists twelve Scotts, but there is only one Caine. Many years later, as one of the hosts at the 1972 Oscar ceremony, he announced, 'If it hadn't been for an American film called *The Caine Mutiny,* the bloke standing before you would still be called Maurice Micklewhite.'

While his acting career chugged along in bottom gear, he supplemented his income by working as a washer-up in the kitchens of a Jermyn Street restaurant, as a plumber's mate, as a hotel night clerk, as a maker of cardboard jewellery boxes. He loaded individual fruit pies at Lyons Corner House, and pushed trucks around a Brixton steam laundry, but all the time he was trudging round agents and examining the columns of *The Stage.*

His wife became pregnant. Shortly after the birth of their

daughter, Dominique, she issued her husband with an ultimatum – get a steady job, or get out. He got out. The marriage had lasted two and a half years. Dominique was brought up by Patricia's parents, in Sheffield, and would one day make a name for herself in showjumping. Five years later, Patricia would marry again and afterwards fielded queries about her ex-husband with good grace.

Caine was still reeling from the break-up of his marriage when his father died from cancer of the liver. Although the illness had been long, Caine was devastated. Mr Micklewhite had never been entirely happy with the idea of his son becoming an actor, but he had grown to accept it. Mrs Micklewhite, meanwhile, had backed her eldest son to the hilt, presenting him with her life savings to help him through the rough patches, and now she gave him the twenty-five pounds she had collected in insurance money and suggested he seek out a change of scenery. He took the ferry to Paris, where he stayed for six months, doing odd jobs, sleeping rough or on the floor of people's flats. At school he had always been good at French; now he was able to put it to use, and one day, he would be able to chat to Brigitte Bardot in her native language. Surviving in Paris was a challenge, and it helped put him back on his feet.

He returned to London and applied himself with a new vigour to the fashioning of a career. Much of it consisted of hanging around in agents' offices, but in 1956 he appeared in his first feature film, *A Hill in Korea,* a war story starring Harry Andrews, George Baker and – a man who would later help to boost him into the big time – Stanley Baker. Caine, as a private, was unbilled, and he remained unbilled in *Sailor Beware!* and *The Steel Bayonet* – both appearances of the blink-and-you'll-miss-him variety. At last, in *How to Murder a Rich Uncle,* he received a credit for his role as an Irish gangster (having beaten another unknown actor called Sean Connery to the part), but most of his lines were cut or redistributed to leading man Nigel Patrick.

He was uncredited again as a POW in *Carve Her Name With Pride*; was cut from the final print of *The Key,* directed by Carol Reed, after the special effects explosion in his scene failed to come up to snuff; had a couple of lines in *Blind Spot* but didn't make the credits; nor did he make them in *The Two-Headed Spy, Passport to Shame,* and *Danger Within.* But he had lines *and* billing in *Foxhole in Cairo,* in which he played a German soldier.

In *The Bulldog Breed,* he was one of the sailors who rescue Norman Wisdom from Oliver Reed and his teddy boy friends, after which Norman joins the Navy – leading to the classic comic scene (well, one of my friends laughed so much his parents had to remove him from the cinema) in which his diver's suit accidentally gets pumped full of air. He can be spotted in the prototype disaster movie *The Day the Earth Caught Fire* as a policeman, saying, 'Keep moving please, down to the Embankment – this district is out of bounds,' though again he is absent from the credits. He played another Irish gangster in the Edgar Wallace adaptation *Solo for Sparrow,* though his Irish accent was apparently so unconvincing he ended up with only a few of his original lines intact. And he played another uncredited policeman in the Peter Sellers comedy *The Wrong Arm of the Law.*

Throughout the late Fifties and into the early Sixties, he had been making sporadic appearances on television: occasional small parts in *Dixon of Dock Green* and *The Adventures of William Tell*; as a court orderly in his namesake play, *The Caine Mutiny Court Martial*; as an uncredited boxer in *Requiem for a Heavyweight,* which featured a little-known actor called Sean Connery as Mountain McClintock; small roles in *No Hiding Place, Mark Saber* and assorted Plays of the Week and Sunday Night Theatres; a photographer here and a third policeman there. In 1961, he played one of the roles in a Johnny Speight two-hander called *The Compartment*; Frank Finlay was the middle-class businessman terrorised on a train by Caine's young thug. His TV roles were gradually getting bigger, he was getting himself noticed at last and was offered a regular role on a new police series then in the planning stage: *Z Cars.* He turned it down. 'I just felt that a long television run was a dead cert short cut to oblivion as an actor,' he said later. Michael Caine was still gunning for a career in movies. He was now approaching his thirtieth birthday.

Caine's years in the galleys were tougher than most. He was no overnight sensation, that's for sure. For those fortunate to spend their lives sailing from one job to another, being showered with opportunities, it is almost impossible to imagine the hardships and anxiety involved in trying to scrape a career together out of nothing, living from hand to mouth on a succession of badly paid jobs which appear to be leading nowhere. Caine's determination during this period must have been awesome. No wonder he found it hard to stop working later on, when he no longer had to worry about earning a living. Even when he'd made it as a movie star, he would still be making films at the rate of two or three a year. 'I still have that feeling that I must carry on, whatever my accountant says,' he would later confess. 'I know it's improbable that I will ever again be on my uppers, scratching for bread. But I believe that with my mind, not with my heart or my instinct.' After launching his professional acting career in repertory, Caine's subsequent theatrical forays took third place to his attempts to break into film and television. In 1958, he had a small role with Sam Wanamaker's Liverpool-based company, playing a sailor in *One More River*, starring Robert Shaw. For three months he was understudy to Peter O'Toole as Sergeant Bamforth in the acclaimed West End production of *The Long and The Short and The Tall*. Terence Stamp, in the second part of his autobiography, describes O'Toole operating at full throttle, legless and screaming for Fernet Branca until he hit the stage, when he would instantly become stone-cold professional; there were a lot of close calls, but he never missed a performance.

When O'Toole went off to play Lawrence of Arabia in David Lean's film of the same name, Caine took over the role for a six-month tour of the provinces; the revised cast included Frank Finlay and Roy Kinnear and was later joined by the unknown Stamp, who had painstakingly learned a Geordie accent for his role, and assumed during rehearsals that the actor playing Bamforth was speaking fake Cockney. Stamp described Caine as 'a strapping young man with a head of unruly blond curls' and reckoned his eyes were his most arresting feature; they were 'large, hooded and blue' with a slightly myopic quality. Stamp, of course, is also well-known for his piercing blue eyes, which can be an invaluable asset for a film actor; Paul Newman's got them, so has Peter O'Toole. Steve McQueen had them. Brown eyes are two a penny, but everyone remembers blue. 'In the theatre, you never see the eyes,' said Caine, 'and in the movies, that is about all you ever see.'

Once Caine and Stamp had recognised each other as genuine East Enders, they started hanging around together. Caine, who by now was becoming an old hand at the acting game, showed Stamp the ropes on tour and later helped him get the hang of a Bristol dialect for his film debut in Peter Ustinov's *Billy Budd*. Back in London, they shared digs in Marylebone before moving to a flat in Knightsbridge. The team split up in 1964, when Caine found a new flat in Marble Arch. According to Stamp, he and his new girlfriend, Jean Shrimpton, decided they were not being made welcome. Probably it was the presence of Shrimpton which put the kibosh on the happy bachelor twosome; Caine would later ask a journalist not to reveal the whereabouts of his home, 'or all the birds will be flocking there again. I had a lot of trouble when I was sharing a flat with Terry Stamp.'

In 1960, Caine appeared at the Royal Court in a play called *The*

Room, written by an actor who had appeared in *The Long and The Short and The Tall* under the stage name of David Baron; his real name was Harold Pinter. Caine finally made his West End debut in January of 1963, as the Cockney narrator of *Next Time I'll Sing To You,* a play based on the real-life story of a man who lived for the last forty-four years of his life as a recluse. It doesn't sound like the most riveting premise for a drama, but the play was a great success, and Caine attracted favourable attention from some of the critics. He shared a dressing room with Barry Foster and Michael Bryant, who couldn't believe it when he told them he hated the theatre and was going to be a film-star.

In February of that year, he was offered a part in a film called *Zulu.*

2

ZULU

Before *Zulu,* Michael Caine was just another face in the crowd. After *Zulu,* he was a movie-star in the ascendant. The role which cracked it for him bore no relation to anything he'd played before; it was a world away from all those Irish gangsters and policemen, anonymous army privates and naval ratings, young thugs and assorted Londoners. Who in a million years would have predicted that Michael Caine in his breakthrough performance would be playing a toff?

'Casting me in *Zulu* was absurd, on the face of it,' Caine would say later. 'But they wanted someone who looked upper class and yet wouldn't appear too much of a nit. So I got the part.' He had originally attended casting sessions for *Zulu* with an eye on being selected for one of the Cockney roles, preferably the plum one of Private Henry Hook, apparently an insolent layabout who nevertheless proves he is in possession of the right stuff when the assegais are out – a part which must have seemed tailor-made for Caine, who had perfected his own brand of insolence as a private in the armed forces. But it turned out the role had already been promised to James Booth.

Caine read for several minor roles before the director asked him if he could do an upper-class accent. Caine switched quickly into Old Etonian mode and said, 'Why, Mr Endfield, I've been doing it for years.' It was decided to try him out as Lieutenant Gonville Bromhead, a product of the officer class whose father fought at Waterloo – a meaty role comprising fifty-two lines of dialogue, lots of close-ups, plenty of reaction shots, a dash of Victoria Cross-winning heroics and prominent billing in the credits. He was screen-tested, but heard nothing more until he ran into the director at a party and learned the screen test had been terrible. But, he was told, 'You've got the part because we're leaving on Monday and we can't find anyone else.' It was in the nick of time. According to Terence Stamp, Caine had resolved to pack away his acting ambitions if he hadn't made significant progress before his thirtieth birthday. The party took place on the evening of 13 March, 1963, and Michael Caine turned thirty at midnight.

'They wanted someone who looked upper class and yet wouldn't appear too much of nit.' Caine as Lt Bromhead in **Zulu**

It is hard to imagine a director of the old-school British type envisaging a working-class actor with a London accent in the role of an aristocratic officer, but Cyril Raker Endfield, known as Cy, was of a more cosmopolitan persuasion, a man whose skills ranged from conjuring tricks to the invention of a miniature computerised typewriter. Born in South Africa and brought up in America, he had been forced out of Hollywood by the House Un-American Activities Committee and resumed his film-making career in Britain. One of the films he wrote and directed was *Hell Drivers,* a rubber-burning action thriller starring Stanley Baker as an ex-convict trucker. Baker, of rugged Welsh stock, was the first British screen actor to convey what the film critic David Thomson refers to as 'proletarian male vigour' as opposed to the more genteel qualities of the theatrical knights. Once Baker's film-acting career was established, he expanded into production; in all he produced four films, two with Endfield, of which *Zulu* was the first.

There is something about a big battle movie that is capable of stirring the blood of the most ardent pacifist – from the comfort of a cinema seat, the filmgoer can sample the heady combination of disaster movie, history lesson and flag-waving folly with minimal risk to life or limb. Big battle movies are thin on the ground these days. With run-of-the-mill action films regularly costing thirty or forty million dollars, period pictures featuring lots of scrupulously drilled extras and explosive pyrotechnics are prohibitively expensive. There is also the moral dilemma of how to present the spectacle of thousands of men making mincemeat of each other. Should it be viewed as a noble, glorious pursuit, or as a tragic, meaningless waste of life – or as a bit of both? Added to which, one imagines, is the consideration that one man's deadly enemy is another man's box-office; overseas markets are a vital factor in today's film financing, but there can't be too many foreign filmgoers who enjoy watching their ancestors being reduced to a load of non-speaking extras whose sole function is to be deep-sixed by heroic Imperialist thugs.

Back in the early Sixties, no-one worried about such things. New Waves were in the offing, but Hollywood was still lording it over international cinema, just as Britain had once queened it over the Empire, and the rest of the world had to take what Hollywood decided to offer. The film industry continued to reel from mass audience defections to television, but cinema was fighting back with the sort of spectacle you just wouldn't be able to squeeze into a small box. Widescreen epics – *Spartacus, El Cid, Cleopatra, The Fall of the Roman Empire* – were in their heyday, and most of them managed to pack in a battle or two.

Zulu didn't reach back quite so far into the mists of history for its story. On 22 January 1879, at Isandhlwana in Zululand, six companies of the British army were overwhelmed by an enormous army (or *impi*) of Zulu warriors led by Cetshwayo, nephew of the late, great Shaka, the first Zulu king. More than thirteen hundred British soldiers lost their lives, though military historians tend to overlook the Zulu fatalities, which numbered over two thousand. Nevertheless, when one considers that the British were fighting with guns and the Zulus with spears, it was a great victory for the home team, and a kick in the teeth for those gentlemen of the Empire who thought British troops could walk all over uncivilised native rabble. The engagement and its outcome were in many ways similar to General Custer's blunder at Little Big Horn in 1876; in both cases, the heavily outnumbered white invaders split their forces and were scuppered by a combination of complacency, rotten judgement and incompetence. A decisive factor in the British collapse at Isandhlwana was a failure in the supply of ammunition; there was plenty of it available, but in boxes secured with metal bands each held in place by six screws – and there were only two screwdrivers in the entire camp.

Shortly after the massacre, an impi of four thousand Zulu descended on the Oscarberg mission station at Rorke's Drift where a hundred and thirty-nine British officers and men (thirty-five of them hospital cases even before the fighting started) withstood repeated onslaughts throughout the night. The Britons lost seventeen men. More than three hundred and fifty Zulus died. *Zulu* is the story of that twelve-hour battle.

The original story was written by John Prebble, who also co-wrote the screenplay with Endfield. Prebble had already written his book *Culloden* (later to be made into a memorable television film), about the English rout of the rebellious Highlanders in 1746, demonstrating the same fierce sympathy for the fighting man which gives *Zulu* much of its backbone. The writers strike a deft balance, steering clear of excessive glory-mongering while refusing to belittle the heroism. In 1979 the massacre at Isandhlwana was commemorated in a very inferior prequel called *Zulu Dawn*, in which Endfield, as co-writer, falls into most of the clichés which he and Prebble had earlier managed to avoid. Nowadays, *Zulu Dawn* is consigned to the dustbin of film history, while *Zulu* stands up surprisingly well, even if, from a white liberal middle-class point of view, one is left with a few white liberal middle-class misgivings. The odds might have been nearly forty to one at Rorke's Drift, but, hell, spears can do only so much against trained riflepower, and somewhere at the back of the brain is the niggling, spoilsport feeling that the British should never have been mucking about in Natal in the first place, let alone marching into neighbouring Zululand.

Despite all that, you have to take your hat off to the plucky troops holed up in the mission station as they stand firm before the enemy, whose approach in the film is heralded by a sound resembling a distant steam train. Besides, it makes for truly spectacular and exciting action, and the Zulus are given due credit as a formidable fighting force, capable of covering vast distances on foot, forming themselves into the shape of an ox, and surrounding their enemy with a deadly pincer movement of the horns. However, the film kicks off with a burst of local colour worthy of *National Geographic.* It depicts a grand wedding ceremony which at least hints that the Zulus are a people with a day-to-day existence beyond the confines of the story, rather than merely cannon fodder for the heroes to mow down.

The film divides its time quite democratically between officers and men, paying special attention to the eleven soldiers who were later to be awarded the Victoria Cross – Chard, Bromhead and Hook amongst them. Most of the troops defending Rorke's Drift were Welshmen, which goes some way towards explaining Stanley Baker's interest in the project. Baker himself played Lt John Chard of the Royal Engineers, whose blue uniform was exchanged for cinematic purposes for the more picturesque red one worn by everyone else.

As Hook, James Booth never set foot in South Africa; all his scenes were shot back in London, so he could continue to act in the Royal Shakespeare Company production of *King Lear* at the Aldwych, and his appearances do appear to be set apart from the rest of the film – most of them are indoors, for a start, and he never shares the screen with Baker or Caine.

Caine's research informed him that in real life Bromhead had been short, dark and semi-deaf. It would have been easy to present him as 'a wishy-washy upper-crust Victorian officer,' as Caine put it, but he was determined not to fall into this trap. He may be the sort of chap who says, 'chin chin' and 'old boy', but Caine persuaded Baker and Endfield to let him play the role as stronger than written by suggesting to them that it would reflect better on Baker's character if he were jostling for command with an officer who was less of an upper-class twit, more Chard's equal.

The first time we catch sight of Caine he is out on a hunting expedition. Or rather, we see a long shot of a pony bearing a propman standing in for Caine, who had started to do the shot and fallen off. The pony, accustomed to the flatness of the plains, was unused to hills and had reared up at the sight of its own shadow. For the actor, it was to be the first of several unfortunate encounters with the horse or its four-legged friend, the camel.

Baker, as Lt John Chard, ends up in command thanks to his seniority over Bromhead, but his performance is strangely muted; perhaps he was preoccupied with his role as co-producer. But he leaves the field clear for Caine, who seizes his opportunity. He based his character partly on the platoon commander from his National Service days and partly on the Duke of Edinburgh, walking with his hands clasped behind his back. And he spoke softly, having already observed that people born into privileged backgrounds take it for granted that everyone will listen to what they have to say. To help with the accent, Baker had arranged for him to visit the officers' mess of the Scots Guards at Pirbright. 'Afterwards some people said they thought I'd overdone the accent, slurring the vowels and that,' Caine said. 'But they do, those people. That's how they talk.'

With hindsight Bromhead looks exactly like Michael Caine giving a performance as a man with an upper-class accent, but he also looks like a star, no question. The camera loves him. Already he knows how to steal the show by underplaying, though it must be difficult to underplay it when most of the action dictates that you run around yelling at the top of your voice. If the accent sounds phoney now, it's only because we're accustomed to the sound of his real voice.

Caine knew it was make-or-break time. When he first saw the *Zulu* rushes, he was so nervous he was sick on the floor – and he never went to see rushes again. For about a year after making *Zulu,* he continued to do television work, though now he was being cast in bigger roles. He played Horatio in the BBC's 1964 production of *Hamlet at Elsinore,* in which the title role was taken by Christopher Plummer (another Canadian, Donald Sutherland, played Fortinbras, and the cast also included Robert Shaw as Claudius and Roy Kinnear as the Grave Digger). Caine also played the lead in a play for Granada Television, *The Other Man,* co-starring Sian Phillips and John Thaw. With the exception of an Alun Owen play in 1969, that was Michael Caine's last television appearance until 1988.

In the meantime, there were movies. Lots and lots of movies.

3

HARRY PALMER

It wasn't until 1965, when he read the reviews of *The Ipcress File* that Michael Caine knew he'd finally made it.

The Sixties were the decade of the Secret Agent. The Cold War was at its chilliest, and the British people decided, in the wake of the Profumo scandal and Kim Philby's defection to Moscow, that authority was not to be trusted. Spies were anti-establishment mods; the look was as important as the lifestyle. The great spy craze lifted workaday paranoia into the heights of surrealism with a plethora of daft code-names, hi-tech headquarters sequestered behind seedy shopfronts, and gadgets masquerading as everyday hardware. It was an era of the Great National Stereotype: the Americans wore white hats, the Russians wore black hats, and the British wore bowler hats and carried umbrellas. But there were bad apples in every barrel; nobody is to be taken at face value, nothing is what it seems. Your table-lamp could be a bugging device; your best friend could be a double-agent; the working-class Cockney who lives down the road could suddenly reveal himself to be a famous film-star.

On television: *Danger Man, The Man from UNCLE, The Saint, The Avengers, Callan, The Prisoner.* On the printed page: Ian Fleming, John Le Carré, Peter O'Donnell, Len Deighton. And on the big screen: Sean Connery as James Bond, Dean Martin as Matt Helm and James Coburn as Derek Flint. The Secret Agent Man held sway.

The spy craze coincided with what looked suspiciously like a British film boom. Hammer horror was still going strong. Beatlemania, and its attendant box-office, had hit the big screen with *A Hard Day's Night*, and Beatles' director Richard Lester's running-jumping-and-standing-still style had permeated the media. Meanwhile, pop realism had reared its warty head in *Saturday Night and Sunday Morning, A Kind of Loving* and *This Sporting Life.* American companies liked what they saw (and what they saw had dollar signs stamped all over it) and began to pour money into the British film industry.

'I don't mind glasses, actually. I can hide behind them.' Harry Palmer in Face Furniture; **The Ipcress File**

By the end of 1964, Canadian-born, American-based producer

Harry Saltzman had already produced, with Albert R Broccoli, three phenomenally successful Bond films. Now he was looking for the flipside to Bond, and found him in the nameless hero of Len Deighton's novel *The Ipcress File.* Christopher Plummer was up for the role, but dropped out to make *The Sound of Music.* Caine's agent, Dennis Selinger, pointed Saltzman in the right direction, setting up a meeting at one of the actor's favourite haunts. Saltzman introduced himself and said, 'You look like a man with three balls.' Ten minutes later, Caine was signed up on an exclusive seven-year contract.

Since Deighton's hero had no name, one had to be picked for the film. Saltzman summoned his leading actor to a meeting with the director and distributors in Wardour Street, and asked them to come up with 'a common or garden name that means absolutely nothing at all.' Caine committed a slight *faux pas* by suggesting Harry.

Harry Palmer was designed as the antithesis of James Bond – the glamorous secret agent with superman skills, a jet-setting lifestyle and a girl (or two, or three, or four) in every airport. 'We're not after worship,' said Caine. 'We're after empathy. This is a spy's spy . . . Definitely sweaty as opposed to glossy.' He reckoned that, in the unlikely event of the two spies meeting each other, Palmer would have regarded Bond as a bit of a toffee-nosed twit. He described the match as 'rather like a Cockney tearaway, who hasn't had any boxing training, coming up against the heavyweight champion from Cambridge.'

The opening credits sequence of *The Ipcress File* lays down the ground rules. An alarm clock goes off, and we see Harry Palmer getting up in the morning. The first thing he does is put on his glasses.

'I'm short-sighted. That's why I wear glasses,' Caine told the *Sunday Express*. 'I don't mind glasses, actually. I can hide behind them. And birds seem to like them.' Sitting in the audience as a teenager, he had always dreamed of seeing a film-star 'who had an Achilles Heel, like being short-sighted'.

He was the first leading man to wear spectacles since the silent comedian Harold Lloyd. Before Harry Palmer, spectacles were a prop for disguise, shorthand for ugly, or the sign that a normally glamorous star was pretending to be an eccentric academic or a plain secretary; it was an established cliché that when bespectacled characters fell in love, they cast aside their face furniture and became . . . *beautiful.* Cary Grant wore glasses when he played the absentminded professor in *Bringing Up Baby.* In *How to Marry a*

The Cockney cup of tea; Harry Palmer in **The Ipcress File**

Millionaire, myopic Marilyn Monroe prefers to blunder into walls rather than risk appearing unattractive in spectacles. Even in Hollywood today, little has changed; Woody Allen is a comic neurotic, Darryl Hannah wears spectacles to denote serious character acting as opposed to bimbo posturing in *Steel Magnolias,* and Julia Roberts peers through a pair in *Flatliners* to indicate she is not just a pretty woman but an incredibly brainy medical student. But action heroes *never* wore glasses until Harry Palmer. When he takes his off, it is an indication that, one way or another, he means business. He tucks them into his breast pocket as the prelude to a fight. And when leading lady Sue Lloyd asks him if he always wears spectacles, he replies, 'Yes, except in bed.' She promptly removes them.

Specs in place, Harry Palmer turns to his next morning task – boiling a kettle and making coffee. This is a favourite mundane task for a film character to engage in. Screenwriter William Goldman, in his book *Adventures in the Screen Trade,* describes how he thought up a credits sequence for *Harper* (which came out not long after *The Ipcress File*) in which Paul Newman, as private eye Lew Archer, recycles his used coffee grounds. Even in the 1982 *film noir* spoof *Dead Men Don't Wear Plaid,* much mileage is squeezed out of Steve Martin's coffee recipe (complete with eggshells). Coffee-making equals downbeat, almost deadbeat. You never saw James Bond making coffee. And you never saw James Bond waking up *alone.*

Observation duties, filling in forms; the workaday facts of Harry Palmer's life are rapidly sketched in. At the start of the film, if not the whole way through, he's just like any other £24-a-week man, except that he happens to be a spy. Bond always had unlimited funds which he could fritter away at the gaming tables, but when Palmer is transferred to another department, his boss promises him a hundred pound rise to take his salary up to £1400 – hardly a fortune, even in those days. 'Oh thank you sir,' says Palmer, deadpan. 'Now I can get that new infra-red grill.' In common with Deighton, his creator, Palmer is a gourmet and a nifty cook; his bedsitter is small and spartan, but there are telltale copper pans and a string of onions hanging on the kitchen wall. We see him impressing his ladyfriend by breaking two eggs into a bowl at once (this rather tricky stunt was doubled by Deighton himself), and his idea of romantic foreplay is telling her, 'I . . . am going to cook you . . . the best meal . . . you've ever eaten.' There is also a splendid sequence – mostly improvised – in which Palmer and his boss (Colonel Ross, the pigeon feeder, played in all three Harry Palmer films by Guy

The spectacle set: Len Deighton and Caine on location for **Funeral in Berlin.**

Doleman) meet in a supermarket and discuss button mushrooms before getting down to serious spycatching. An interest in food, in a nation which has always been notoriously indifferent to it, is more than enough to mark out Harry Palmer as exotic and unusual.

Palmer is not the patriotic sort, and is certainly not risking his neck for Queen and Country. James Bond's approach may sometimes be unorthodox but, unlike Palmer, he could never be described as insubordinate, or as a trickster with criminal tendencies. Palmer is a reluctant secret agent, ex-army; he has become a spy in preference to being locked up in a military prison for unspecified offences on the black market.

The word 'Ipcress' derives from 'Induction of Psychoneuroses by Conditioned Reflex under strESS'. British scientists are defecting, selling-out or losing their memory en masse, it seems, after exposure to the enemy's radical conditioning techniques. To avoid being framed for the murder of a CIA agent who has been tailing him, Palmer makes a break for the continent, runs straight into the arms of the bad guys, and wakes up to find himself in an Albanian prison cell. After several days without food, he is given the treatment – this consists of his being locked in a metal box where he is bombarded with ear-splitting *Dr Who*-style music (Palmer, we already know, prefers Mozart) and what look like College of Art slide shows until his willpower cracks and he apparently succumbs to hypnotic suggestion. When he finally manages to escape, he is immediately confronted by a Routemaster bus and a red telephone booth which inform him that he is in Tourist London, not Albania after all. Palmer's insolence pays off in the end, when he is confronted by two men, one of whom is a traitor; more out of bloody-mindedness than anything else, he manages to resist his brainwashing and shoot the double-agent.

The real antidote to Bond was probably not Harry Palmer but Richard Burton as the hero of John Le Carré's *The Spy Who Came In From the Cold,* a relentlessly downbeat spy thriller which was released the same year as *Ipcress.* In retrospect, *The Ipcress File* doesn't come across as an antidote to the gadget-packed Bond films so much as a complement to them; nowadays it looks every bit as far-fetched and unrealistic as *Dr No* or *The Silencers.* It trades on pop realism. The settings are so drab they become picturesque; a raid on an empty warehouse becomes almost abstract, as do the offices full of cigarette smoke, and an exchange which takes place in that staple thriller location, the underground car-park.

The unabashed use of London landmarks – the Albert Hall, Trafalgar Square, the Science Museum – seems to belong to a happier,

more confident age when one of the lateral functions of a flourishing British film industry was to cater to an international market of potential tourists. Canadian-born Sidney J Furie's direction is all odd camera angles and gimmicky shooting through car windows and telephone booths. This might have been annoying and artsy at the time, but now it appears charmingly quirky and Sixties-ish, and succeeds in disguising the rather sedentary nature of much of the plot; seldom can so many characters in what is ostensibly an action film have spent so much time talking on the telephone.

Caine in his second big role – and the first in which he was able to air his London accent – was outstanding, striking the perfect balance between character acting and star performance which has been his province ever since. The scene in which he answers the phone and learns of the murder of a colleague is a case study in Pudovkin technique: he receives the news (which we can't hear, though we know what it is) with a barely perceptible flare of the nostrils and a slight movement of the eyeballs.

'Someone once said of Harry Palmer that he is a winner who came on like a loser,' said Caine. 'I liked that – you could say the same of me.' After *The Ipcress File,* Caine donned the famous Harry Palmer spectacle frames twice more before the series tailed off; he had originally been signed for a five-film run but Saltzman let him out of the deal. There was talk of hunting for another actor to play the secret agent in a fourth Palmer film, *Horse Under Water,* adapted from another Len Deighton story, but the idea fizzled out. Michael Caine *was* Harry Palmer, it was a character he had made his own, and anyone else in the role would have been a non-starter. 'I won't be wearing spectacles on the screen again,' he told the *Daily Mail,* 'unless they are an essential part of the story.'

In *Funeral in Berlin* (1966), Palmer is sent to sound out Colonel Stok, a Soviet intelligence officer who has let it be known he wants to defect. Palmer is still a gourmet ('You're useless in the kitchen,' he tells a girlfriend, 'why don't you go back to bed?'), his boss is still feeding pigeons from the window of his Trafalgar Square office. But whereas Sidney J Furie had given *The Ipcress File* a non-naturalistic feel with his lunatic camera angles, director Guy Hamilton keeps *Funeral* functional and rather drab. (Perhaps Hamilton, who directed several Bond movies, was trying too hard to provide an unglamorous, unexciting contrast.) Once we swap the red London Routemasters for the Berlin Wall, the plot strangles itself on a surfeit of twists, incorporating an old pal of Palmer's from his black market days, and some vengeful Zionists who are trying to track down money plundered from Jews during the war. There is a fake

Six years before he was compared to 'soggy oatmeal', Caine has a close call with a box of cornflakes; **Billion Dollar Brain**

funeral, and Palmer's old pal turns out to be a Nazi, but the audience is left confused, bemused, and – unfortunately – insufficiently amused.

What amusement value there is stems mostly from the central character and his accessories, though there is also an enjoyably bluff performance from Oscar Homolka as the defecting Russian, Colonel Stok. Caine's Harry Palmer is as watchable as ever, and he delivers a stream of deadpan one-liners with impeccable comic timing. 'I like England,' says a curvaceous Euro-cutie to whom he has been introduced. Pause. 'England likes you,' says Harry Palmer. Caine can even deliver a groan-making oldie as if it were crisp and new. 'Bitte, mein Herr,' says a passing waiter. 'No,' says Harry, 'Lowenbrau please.'

Fashion note: Harry Palmer has a seemingly inexhaustible supply of trendy car-coats and shorty mackintoshes. In fact, one of his raincoats ends up as an important meaningful prop; when Harry's treacherous friend puts it on in an attempt to disguise himself, he is immediately mistaken for Harry and shot dead by the Zionists.

Caine played Palmer for a third and final time in *Billion Dollar Brain* (1967), a much more flamboyant affair than either of its two predecessors, probably because it was directed by Ken Russell. Though this was only his second full-length feature, he had already made his mark in television and was shaping up to become the

The Billion Dollar Brain in action, left. Ways of keeping warm in a Cold War climate, right; Caine and Oscar Homolka knock back the Vodka in **Billion Dollar Brain**

enfant terrible of the British film industry. *Billion Dollar Brain* is by far the best of the Palmer movies, though neither critics nor audiences liked it at the time. The story is confusing, certainly, but served up with a panache that was nowhere to be seen in the equally confusing *Funeral in Berlin.* It is the sort of plot which would probably be deemed acceptable if it were set entirely in a suite of beige-coloured offices, but Russell's cinematic flair, for some reason, tends to upset critics, who seem to regard it as unsporting, even *un-British.* The plot is years ahead of its time, anticipating *glasnost* in its teaming of East and West united against a common foe, in this case a Texan millionaire whose rabid anti-communism seems set to trigger World War Three. Deighton, who was one of the first writers to switch from a typewriter to a word-processor, also anticipates Stanley Kubrick's *2001: A Space Odyssey* with the billion dollar brain itself, a gigantic computer which like HAL has a distinct personality of its own.

Harry Palmer has left the British Secret Service to start his own detective agency, but his old boss, Colonel Ross, soon blackmails him back into the fold. Palmer is assigned to deliver a thermos flask containing a set of lethal viruses to an old friend in Helsinki, who turns out to be working for the mad Texan millionaire. No sooner has Harry got to Finland than he is shivering in his mackintosh and has to swap it for a more suitable double-breasted overcoat with a fur collar and matching hat. Anti-fur campaigners might well want to throw red paint at the screen during this film, because few of the actors are to be seen without a very fetching array of fur headgear.

When he realises what the Texan is up to, Palmer pools resources with his old chum Colonel Stok (a welcome reappearance by Oscar Homolka), and the film climaxes with the forces of anti-communism drowning in the Baltic as the ice cracks around them – a homage to the Battle on the Ice at the end of Sergei Eisenstein's *Alexander Nevsky*, a famous sequence though evidently not as famous as the same director's massacre on the Odessa Steps in *Battleship Potemkin*, which has been parodied in everything from Terry Gilliam's *Brazil* to Brian De Palma's *The Untouchables*.

Caine's brother, Stanley, plays the postman who delivers the fatal thermos flask to Palmer's office at the beginning of the film. Female interest is provided by the very wonderful Françoise Dorléac, Catherine Deneuve's older sister, who plays the cello very badly and tries to stab Harry Palmer with a long pin. *Billion Dollar Brain* was Dorléac's second British spy movie; she had already appeared with David Niven in *Where the Spies Are*, adapted from a novel by James Leasor, and she is several cuts above the usual dollybirds who draped themselves over secret agents in the Sixties. *Billion Dollar Brain*, unfortunately, was her last film. In June 1967, before shooting had been completed, she went to visit her sister in the South of France. Driving fast to catch a plane from Nice airport, she skidded into a signpost and died when her car caught fire.

Maurice Binder, best known as the creator of the gun-barrel view of 007 preceding every Bond film, assembled one of his very finest credit sequences for *Billion Dollar Brain*, incorporating computer keyboards, filing cabinets and a recurring Michael Caine motif. Binder's visuals and Richard Rodney Bennett's score combine into an intro which gets the adrenalin flowing, something one encounters all too rarely these days; back in the Sixties, you *knew* you were in for a treat when you saw one of these.

Though there are a few scenes set in London, and a rather hallucinatory sequence purporting to be in Texas, most of the film was shot on location in Finland, where Russell and his cinematographer, Billy Williams, exploit every last variation on the photogenic possibilities of snow-covered landscapes and steel-grey skies. What *Billion Dollar Brain* has, which the first two Harry Palmer films lack, is a dreamlike quality which lingers in the memory long after films with more meretricious plotting have faded. The ending carries a kick as well. In the penultimate scene, a fur-wrapped Dorléac leans over to kiss Palmer, but, stung by her treachery, he doesn't respond. Harry Palmer has been hurt – we know this because the normally unblinking Caine blinks several times, and this minimal action carries more emotional weight than any amount of breast-beating and hair-tearing would have done. For the first time, Palmer is showing signs of emotional distress. It is a pity that just as we are starting to suspect he is not as battle-hardened as he seems, the Palmer saga comes to an end and we have to leave him there.

During filming, Caine, who at this stage in his career didn't know any better, found himself doing many of the dangerous stunts that stuntmen usually do. Russell's use of the zoom lens made it impossible for anyone to stand in for the actor. He had Caine jumping from ice floe to ice floe, three miles out on the Baltic Sea, surrounded by water which was minus 50 degrees Centigrade. 'He was very brave,' said Russell. 'I wouldn't have done it.' A Finn on the set afterwards pointed out that the actor should have been equipped with 'ice knives'. Had he fallen into the water, without knives to stick into the ice and haul himself out, he would have been a goner.

In another close call, Caine was supposed to jump aboard a moving train, and noticed just in time that someone had forgotten to scrape the ice from the running board. This was the same year that Zbigniew Cybulski, the 'Polish James Dean' who in 1958 had given such a mesmerising performance in *Ashes and Diamonds,* died while attempting to perform a similar feat on the Wroclaw-Warsaw Express, although not in front of movie-cameras.

Over the years, Caine has wised up to dangerous stunts. During filming of *The Island,* he refused point-blank to swim around in shark-infested waters. His advice to budding film actors is, 'Always have a stunt demonstrated to you before you do it.'

A couple of years later, when Ken Russell was preparing to film *Women in Love,* he offered Caine the choice of one of the leading roles. Caine opted to play Gerald (the role which was eventually taken by Oliver Reed) – but only on condition that Russell cut the nude wrestling scene, destined to become the most infamous, talked-about scene in the finished picture. 'I would never appear nude in a picture,' said Caine, though he seems to have had few inhibitions about taking his shirt off. 'When you're naked you're no longer in control of the situation because people are not looking where you want them to, or listening to what you want them to. They're looking at other things – at your genitals – and the interest has gone out of what you're doing. Therefore you lose the control which is the actor's basic weapon.'

4

THE BIRDS

Alfie is not a good film, but Caine's performance in it is terrific. So terrific, in fact, that it would take him years to shake off the Alfie tag. He did nothing to discourage the public's view of him as a girl-happy swinger; he was fast becoming a favourite with the popular press, and often, in the interviews, it is difficult to work out where Alfie stops and Caine begins. Perhaps he wasn't too sure of the dividing line himself.

The screenplay was based on a radio play by Bill Naughton, and the shade of radio looms large in the talkiness of the script; close your eyes and you wouldn't be missing much – apart from Caine's masterly display, of course. Terence Stamp, who played the role on Broadway, described the role as a monster to learn, 'like Hamlet but with more laughs.' Director Lewis Gilbert pitches it midway between a wacky comedy (incorporating modish Sixties touches such as montages of still photographs) and a kitchen-sink drama, all drab flats and dead-end existences. Alfie is a lad and a half; terrified of responsibility, he spreads himself amongst so many women, treating them so shoddily that he ends up with nobody at all, vaguely dissatisfied but unable to put his finger on the reason for his misgivings. 'What's it all about?' he asks, in the line plucked out and made famous by that ghastly theme song sung by Cher (produced by Sonny) and taken into the hit parade by Cilla Black. And 'What's it all about?' echoed the newspaper headlines whenever there was a new development in the actor's love life offscreen.

The main trouble with the film is that all Alfie's women – with the notable exception of Shelley Winters as a robust Older Woman – are such pathetic specimens that one almost ends up sympathising with Alfie's wayward behaviour. Some of them do wise up, though not before allowing him to treat them like dirt. Julia Foster has a child by him but he neglects her; Jane Asher cooks and cleans but he insults her; and – in the film's most memorable scene – Vivien Merchant uncomplainingly has an illegal abortion and somehow refrains from clobbering him over the head when she cries out in agony and he tries to hush her up. The abortion scene is definitely more downbeat, depressing kitchen-sink than wacky

The abortion scene; Vivien Merchant and Caine in **Alfie**

comedy; it leaves a nasty aftertaste, but then it's meant to; for the rest of the film, Alfie's perky charm comes across as a brittle sham. This scene, and the unsympathetic light it casts on the central character who procures the abortion, was apparently one of the reasons the film role was turned down by Terence Stamp, Laurence Harvey, James Booth and Anthony Newley. 'Girls wouldn't like you if you played a sort of rotter,' said Caine, who nevertheless was about to prove otherwise.

In the end, there are just too many women in Alfie's life – Eleanor Bron, Shirley Anne Field, Millicent Martin each have their episodes as well – and the film collapses beneath the weight of repetition. We would have got the same picture from two or three dalliances; in fact, Caine's performance is so good, we virtually get the picture from his opening monologue. When a character turns to the camera and starts confiding in the audience, like Shirley Valentine or Ferris Bueller, it's a device to get you rooting for someone who is preparing to behave very badly indeed. Talking straight to camera is a difficult trick to pull off, but Caine does it with aplomb. Alfie isn't really developed as a character, but Caine manages to make you believe he is. He presents a front, then gradually strips the layers off to reveal the sad, inadequate personality underneath – a despicable character whom the actor makes curiously sympathetic, simply by refusing to play for easy sympathy. The performance is so funny and truthful that it makes you forget the film doesn't really have a narrative, just a string of interchangeable women whom the story treats in exactly the same offhand way as does its hero. The writer's idea of a perfect relationship – the kind that Alfie is so unfortunate to be missing out on – appears to be one in which he would behave like a loving, concerned husband, and his wife would uncomplainingly cook, clean and present him with babies. In other words, though it condemns Alfie's cavalier attitude to women, it accepts without question that this is the only thing standing between him and nirvana. Settle down with a good wife, and everything will be just dandy.

In his interviews, Caine would sometimes refer to a woman as 'it' rather than 'she', just like Alfie. 'I like all birds,' he told Roderick Mann of the *Sunday Express*, to whom he gave a great number of interviews over the years. 'Within reason, that is,' he added.

Out of his harem of *Alfie* co-stars, Shirley Anne Field offered the most perceptive comment: 'Michael seems to prefer foreign girls, maybe because they don't understand him. He may have the feeling that English girls might find him out. I think he's actually insecure. I don't think he's all that sexy. He's a quiet, rather sweet

Shirley Anne Field looking after Caine's health in **Alfie**

man, not at all like he wants to be.'

But the quiet, rather sweet man was having a whale of a time playing at being Michael Caine, movie-star. He was nicknamed 'The Birdman of Grosvenor Square' and he talked expansively to the papers about his 'bird' philosophy. 'I swing with any bird I fancy,' he said, adding that he only went out with actresses and models, 'because they're the best lookers'. Earlier in his career he had dated Marie Devereux (best known for her voluptuous presence in the 1959 Hammer film *The Stranglers of Bombay*). He dated Edina Ronay (now a well-known fashion designer, but, back in 1968, one of the suede-bikini set in the Hammer production of *Slave Girls*). He dated Luciana Paluzzi (flame-haired Bond-girl seen to advantage in biking leathers in *Thunderball*). And he dated Alexandra Bastedo, one of the extra-sensory crime-fighters in *The Champions* TV series. He dated Bianca de Macias, who would later become better known as Bianca Jagger. He had a more serious fling with Camilla Sparv, a Swedish model whose acting career peaked in 1967 when she provided Euro-cutie back-up for Dean Martin in the Matt Helm film *Murderer's Row*, but as soon as any of the newspapers got carried away and ran the headline 'MICHAEL CAINE TO MARRY', he would get cold feet.

'I'm a hunter,' said Caine. 'It's not difficult, getting birds.' And his mother, with typical Micklewhite forthrightness, commented, 'I get sick of meeting all his different girls.'

5

YUGOSLAV PRIMITIVES

After *Ipcress* and *Alfie*, Caine found he was exactly what he had always wanted to be: a film-star. And now he had to decide what being a film-star entailed. He was going to dress and behave the way he had always thought film-stars should dress and behave. 'A movie-star shouldn't be like the boy next door, I've always felt that,' he said. 'Nobody wants him to be. They want an image of someone they can think about, dress like, talk like. Me, I'm not going around in sweat shirt and jeans. I want to go about in hundred guinea suits and Rolls-Royces.' His own dream had come true, and now he was going to embody that dream for all the other Maurice Micklewhites out there.

Having been broke for so long, now Caine had money he was determined to enjoy it. 'All that stuff about money not making you happy is just propaganda put out by the rich,' he declared. Nor was he shy about telling everyone how much he was getting. 'I'm perfectly happy,' he said shortly before the release of *Billion Dollar Brain*. 'I do a job I used to do for practically nothing and I'm paid £5000 a week . . . I travel first-class and the fares are paid. I stay in the most luxurious hotels and eat in the best restaurants.' Newspaper reporters egged him on, happy to recycle the same old angles about the Cockney lad doing so well for himself. Journalists were constantly describing his home, or possessions – 'expensive tapestries and costly abstract paintings', or 'a Lowry, two Harold Woods, a Piper, some Yugoslav primitives.' *Yugoslav primitives?* Not many people know about them.

But once in a while, Maurice Micklewhite would poke his head out. 'I realise it's not going to last, all this,' he said. 'That's why I'm working so hard.' Even while he was enjoying his money, he was careful to invest some of it wisely. 'You can't drive around town in an endowment policy,' he said, 'but it's better than walking around skint when you're fifty.'

After the swift one-two punch of *The Ipcress File* and *Alfie,* Caine marked time with the period comedy *The Wrong Box,* directed by Bryan Forbes and adapted from a story by Robert Louis Stevenson.

The end of a cat-burgling career; **Deadfall**

I do not much care for the films of Forbes (though I think he was swell as an actor in the Inspector Clouseau film *A Shot in the Dark*), but he once wrote an angry letter calling me a 'trufflehound' after I gave *The Naked Face* a negative review in a magazine, so I must be careful what I say.

The Wrong Box is traditional British light entertainment in the British light entertainment tradition. It features a number of decorative intertitles, rather in the style of silent movies, though these carry blindingly obvious messages such as 'Disaster strikes!', just prior to disaster striking. John Mills and Ralph Richardson are the only two surviving members of a tontine, a group of twenty boys each of whose fathers pooled one thousand pounds. Through the years, the sum has swollen to one hundred and eleven thousand pounds, and now Mills wants to bump off Richardson so he can get his hands on the loot. The cast list reads like a Who's Who of British Comedy. Peter Cook and Dudley Moore play Richardson's adopted nephews who are understandably anxious to preserve his health; Peter Sellers is a sleazy, cat-festooned doctor; Tony Hancock is a bungling detective; Wilfrid Lawson steals the show with a magnificent turn as a decrepit butler.

As a complete contrast to *Alfie,* Caine played John Mills' son Michael Finsbury, in his own words 'a distinctly unpromising medical student with an unrequited passion for the girl next door' or, as the intertitles would have it, 'The girl he worships from afar', who is played by Forbes's wife, Nanette Newman. Caine wears wire-rimmed spectacles and a horizontally-striped tie, bumbles nicely, and is rather sweet. There is a train wreck, an incorrectly identified corpse and a chase which ends up in a graveyard. It is all played so heavily for laughs that it ends up being not terribly funny. Putting some famous comedians on screen in the hope that an audience will fall about at the sight of their faces just isn't good enough.

During filming, Caine had another of his unfortunate encounters with four-legged things. He and Newman were sitting in a Victorian hearse, when the horses pulling it took fright and bolted. Forbes and his wife were full of praise for the actor, who kept a cool head, held on to the reins and eventually managed to calm the animals down.

In 1968, Caine worked with Forbes a second time in *Deadfall,* a po-faced caper movie based on the novel by Desmond Cory. Caine plays a jewel thief called Henry Clarke (this was the sixth film in three years in which he had played a Harry or a Henry – one might as well refer to the Sixties as the Harry Years), who teams up with a

A night off with Giovanni Ralli in **Deadfall**

married couple to rob a multi-millionaire.

The film would have been more fun if it had been more caper and less relationship. Clarke has an affair with the wife (Giovanna Ralli) who turns out to be married to her father (Eric Portman) who turns out to be a homosexual who betrayed his first male lover to the Gestapo. After a twenty-minute robbery sequence it all ends in tears; Caine falls to his death, Portman shoots himself, and Ralli gets carted off by the police.

6

THE CUP OF TEA

Caine liked working with Americans. 'They've given me the breaks,' he said, probably thinking of Cy Endfield and Harry Saltzman (though neither was actually born in the US). 'I'd rather be a fifth-league international name than a big local one anytime.'

He got his first taste of Hollywood with *Gambit,* with a role that had originally been written for Cary Grant, but by 1966 Grant had virtually retired from acting. A decade earlier, however, he had starred with Grace Kelly in Alfred Hitchcock's *To Catch a Thief,* which had all the trademarks of the lighthearted caper movie; exotic location (the French Riviera), smart dialogue and glamorous stars engaged in featherweight criminal activities (ie, nobody gets hurt, though some fabulously wealthy people might lose a few brooches or bracelets). Darker caper movies (people get killed, the criminals fall out) include John Huston's *The Asphalt Jungle* and Stanley Kubrick's *The Killing,* as well as Jules Dassin's 1955 film *Du Rififi Chez les Hommes* (aka *Rififi*), with its hugely influential thirty-minute silent robbery sequence. In 1964, Dassin made the infinitely glossier *Topkapi,* in which the characters rob a museum in Istanbul.

Gambit is a *Topkapi* type of caper; slick, stylish, and not exactly top-heavy in the metaphysical department. Shirley MacLaine, who carried enough clout to choose her own director, was thinking of hiring Sidney J Furie, and after watching *The Ipcress File,* Furie's latest, she decided she wanted Harry Palmer for her leading man.

Alfie was opening in the United States (Caine had to redub himself with a watered-down Cockney accent for the American market) after a brief flurry of controversy. The Motion Picture Association of America was reluctant to grant it a Production Code seal until persuaded the abortion episode was a morally sound scene illustrating the dangers of promiscuous behaviour. *Who's Afraid of Virginia Woolf?* was having similar problems because of its bad language. But the seal was eventually awarded, and the 'Cockney Charmboy' became the talk of the town. The critic of the *New Yorker* declared that 'Michael Caine couldn't play a Cockney if he tried', but the *New York Daily News* hailed him with an article beginning, 'Well, girls, first it was the Beatles and then it was miniskirts, and now see

Michael Caine, movie-star; with Shirley Bassey at the London premiere of **Hurry Sundown**
(Syndication International)

what the British have sent us in the flicks – a cockney lad who's sure to be just our cup of tea.'

By the time the cup of tea had crossed the Atlantic, he also found himself shortlisted for an Oscar for his performance in *Alfie*. The other Best Actor nominees that year were Alan Arkin for *The Russians are Coming! The Russians are Coming!* Richard Burton for *Who's Afraid of Virginia Woolf?*, Steve McQueen for *The Sand Pebbles*, and Paul Scofield for *A Man for All Seasons*. Scofield won, but, like so many actors before and since, Caine professed himself happy just to have been nominated; now, he had *really* arrived. And he relished the opportunity to rub shoulders with the *crème de la crème* of Hollywood royalty – Gloria Swanson, Frank Sinatra, Judy Garland, Dean Martin, Kirk Douglas, Cary Grant . . . It wasn't just Hollywood royalty; in Danny Kaye's kitchen, he bumped into Prince Philip, who greeted him with, 'Hello, it's old Ipcress, isn't it?' Maurice Micklewhite had come a long way from the Elephant and Castle.

Gambit ended up being directed by Ronald Neame, a workmanlike British director whose output has ranged from the acceptable (*The Horse's Mouth,* adapted from the Joyce Cary novel) to the execrable (*Foreign Body,* a 1986 comedy so objectionable it leaves one gasping for the subleties of *Confessions of a Window Cleaner*). He does a fair job here, though. Caine plays another Harry role – Harry Dean, a con-man who enlists the help of Eurasian showgirl MacLaine to steal a priceless Egyptian statuette from the private apartments of millionaire businessman Herbert Lom, whose late wife she resembles. In the first half of the film, which is set in Hong Kong, Caine outlines the robbery plan to MacLaine, who comes across as little more than a dumb broad. In the second half of the film, however, his carefully-laid schemes keep going awry, and the 'dumb broad' has to step in and save the day.

A year later, as a favour to his *Gambit* co-star, Caine went po Paris to play a small role in one of the episodes of *Woman Times Seven,* an excuse for MacLaine to play seven different characters (widow, career woman, mousy wife, socialite and so on) in seven different stories under the direction of Vittorio de Sica of *Bicycle Thieves* fame. Caine appears in the final segment, as a young man who wordlessly follows MacLaine home; she is flattered by his attentions, but in fact he is a private detective hired by her husband to keep tabs on her movements.

In 1967, Caine appeared, without really intending to, in a feature-length documentary entitled *Tonite Let's All Make Love in London,* a

Caine and Shirley MaClaine plot their next move in **Gambit**

collage of interview, pop performance and dancing dollybirds in an impressionistic celebration of Swinging London. Caine wasn't too happy when the film came out; he had agreed to do a filmed interview without knowing what it was going to be used for. But, like it or not, he was now a part of the Swinging London phenomenon. As Harry Palmer in *The Ipcress File* and its offshoots, he had personified the young public's mounting distrust of authority which would eventually reach its most extreme in anti-war demonstrations and student riots. As Alfie, he had been a figurehead of the more relaxed sexual morality. As Michael Caine, and along with the Beatles, Terence Stamp and David Bailey, he was one of the new young stars who seemed to be proving to the world that being working-class was no barrier to success.

Caine worked hard at maintaining the appropriate lifestyle, going to clubs and discos, and squiring glamorous 'birds' around town. But, unlike many other actors of his generation, he was careful not to raise too much hell. He had taken so long to get there, and he wasn't about to throw it all away.

Caine and Jane Fonda have good sax together in **Hurry Sundown**

7

DEEP SOUTH

Otto Preminger was a Personality Director, one of those film-makers whose faces, like those of Eric Von Stroheim and Alfred Hitchcock, are sometimes better known than the stars who appear in their films. His best work includes the 1944 necrophiliac romance *Laura* and the 1959 courtroom drama *Anatomy of a Murder.* He is also remembered as an actor in Billy Wilder's *Stalag 17,* in which he plays the Nazi commandant of the prisoner-of-war camp. He happily courted controversy; with *The Moon is Blue,* which he directed in 1953, he successfully challenged the Motion Picture Production Code by daring to include in the script such hitherto taboo words as 'pregnant' and 'virgin', and two years later, *The Man With the Golden Arm* featured Frank Sinatra as a drug addict. He had a son by the famous striptease artiste Gypsy Rose Lee, and was never shy about promoting himself on chat shows. The shaven-headed, Austrian-born director also had a fearsome reputation when it came to dealing with actors, but Michael Caine disarmed him from the very beginning by saying he didn't want to be shouted at. 'I only shout at bad actors,' protested the director. 'I would never shout at Alfie.'

Hurry Sundown is far below the standard of his best work, but there is much to enjoy and it is hugely entertaining, a sprawling Deep South melodrama somewhere midway between *Written on the Wind* and *Dallas,* only with no oil, seasoned instead with just a pinch of unintentional kitsch. With *Carmen Jones* and *Porgy and Bess,* Preminger had probably provided more employment for black actors in the Fifties than all the other Hollywood directors put together, and there is enough black acting talent on display in *Hurry Sundown* to make one regret that fat black roles were – and still are – the exception rather than the norm. Robert Hooks (an excellent TV actor who only made about half a dozen film appearances) is good as one of the two heroes, and there is also a welcome appearance from Rex Ingram (not to be confused with the film director of the same name) who played De Lawd in the all-black Bible fable *Green Pastures,* and was particularly memorable as the giant Sinbad-stomping genie in the 1940 British film *The Thief of Bagdad.*

Hurry Sundown is set in Georgia, just after the end of the Second World War. The film was actually shot in Louisiana in 1967, and one should perhaps bear in mind that this was a mere three years after the incident in Mississippi, dramatised in Alan Parker's 1988 film *Mississippi Burning,* in which three civil rights workers were shot dead by local racists – nor was this an isolated occurrence; racist passions were running high in the Deep South throughout the Sixties. The producers of *Hurry Sundown* had to obtain special dispensation from their hotel to allow black and white cast members to use the same swimming-pool, and at one stage of the production, the Ku Klux Klan fired a shotgun at Preminger's trailer.

Nowadays the film is primarily of curiosity value because of the offbeat casting of two of its central roles. As the prototype yuppie and property developer Henry Warren, Caine was faced with his biggest challenge to date. Not only did he have to look as though he could play the saxophone convincingly, he also had to speak his lines with a Southern accent ('shoah a do shugah'), and though it sometimes sounds to British ears as though he isn't quite hitting it on the nail, the natives of Baton Rouge were apparently satisfied. Caine's screen wife was Jane Fonda, who had yet to emerge from her sex kitten phase (*Barbarella* was still a year away) into her awesome incarnation as Serious Actress with Dodgy Political Affiliations.

The plot concerns Caine's attempts to get his hands on Hooks' land by fair means or foul so he can build a cannery; naturally, with Burgess Meredith contributing a glorious ranting bigot turn as a racist judge, the means turn out to be more foul than fair. (Meredith and his director had this in common – they both played villains in the *Batman* TV series, Meredith as The Penguin and Preminger as Mr Freeze.) Henry and his wife have a troubled marriage, troubled even further by their six-year-old son, who has not been right in the head since Henry was left to babysit and tied the poor little chap to his crib for a whole day while he went away on business. Every time Caine and Fonda get involved in snogging manoeuvres, their ardour is dampened by the child screaming his head off. Jane works off her frustration by doing suggestive things to her husband's saxophone; Henry Warren is a thwarted musician with dreams of packing it all in and following the hobo trail to California, and if only he had followed his artistic urges instead of succumbing to land-grabbing greed, or so we are led to believe, everything would have turned out just dandy.

Probably the most authentic-sounding Southern accent on offer is that of Faye Dunaway, who has a head start in this department since she was born and educated in Florida. This was to be the year in which Faye broke through into the big time with *Bonnie and Clyde,* but right now, as a working-class wife who lives in a shack, she was having to struggle with lines such as, 'I look like I'm still working as a welder.' She looks like nothing of the sort; she looks like a glamorous actress with mussed-up hair. Twenty years later, playing an alcoholic opposite Mickey Rourke in *Barfly,* she would still look like a glamorous actress with mussed-up hair. Jane Fonda, playing an alcoholic in *The Morning After,* also mussed up her hair and went easy on the make-up, but failed to disguise her aerobic-trim figure. What these actresses tend to forget, when they play poor or dissipated folk, is that poor or dissipated folk haven't just got mussed-up hair, they have also got bad skins, flabby figures, vitamin deficiencies and no cheekbones.

Dunaway's screen husband, and sharing the hero slot with Hooks, is played by John Philip Law, surely one of the most colourless leading men in the history of cinema, who seems to have appeared in nothing but B-movies for the past twenty years, even though B-movies aren't supposed to exist any more. Dunaway and Law are supposed to represent the happy side of family life (they have four moppet-headed children) as opposed to the strained marriage of Caine and Fonda, but one gets the impression that Faye would prefer to smother her boring family in hayseed and fling herself at the Cockney cup of tea for a serious lobe-chewing session.

Caine wonders why he's the only one not wearing a dress in **The Magus**; *Anna Karina, Anthony Quinn and Candice Bergen model this season's skirt lengths*

In the end, Hooks manages to prove his ownership of the land beyond all dispute. Caine is so miffed that he urges the local racists to retaliate, and one of Faye's offspring is killed in a redneck dynamite explosion. Caine, who had been fond of the little chap, shows his remorse by blubbing. Unfortunately, we don't find out whether he subsequently reforms, becomes even more of a racist bigot, or heads west with his horn, because the film ends with the good guys – black *and* white – swarming happily onto the dynamited land which they are now going to have to spend the rest of their lives licking back into shape.

Hurry Sundown deserves to be cherished as a unique instance of Caine playing in a slice of American Gothic. Naturalism would have been out of place here, and he has accordingly ripened his performance by a few notches to complement the melodramatic material. Even so, he looks more laid-back than most of the cast, and has obviously thought hard about ways to give his role some uncalled-for depth. He portrays Henry Warren as more of a sad, weak man than an out-and-out villain. It is an interesting and adventurous role for a leading man like Caine to have taken on. 'Villainy doesn't exist outside of books or movies,' he said to a reporter during filming. 'In real life men are not heroes or villains, but both at the same time.'

Back in 1965, Caine had seen the film of John Fowles's *The Collector,* starring his ex-flatmate Terence Stamp, and had expressed interest in appearing in the film version of whatever the author happened to write next. He said he would do it, no matter what it was, as part of a two-picture contract with 20th Century Fox (the other film was *Deadfall*). 'They told me it would all come right in the cutting room,' he said afterwards. 'But it didn't.' *The Magus* is a film of legendary badness, causing Woody Allen to swear that, if he were given the chance to live his life over again, he would do everything the same except he wouldn't go and see *The Magus.*

John Fowles's novel was cult stuff in the late Sixties and early Seventies. 'When I read the book,' Caine said, 'I was absolutely fascinated by it.' Even as late as 1984, Yale graduate and film actress Jodie Foster was saying it was her favourite work of fiction. It's the sort of quasi-mystical experience which can seem terribly meaningful while you are reading it, but which afterwards can leave you with the impression of having been taken in by a skilful conjuring trick – there is definitely less there than meets the eye. Anyway, cult books – especially cult films with non-linear narratives – are notoriously difficult to transpose on to the screen successfully, as a glance at the 1990 box-office takings of *The Sheltering Sky* or *The Bonfire of the Vanities* will confirm. The fans of a cult book tend to be extremely possessive; they have their own, very precise ideas of who should or shouldn't be cast in the various roles, and they don't take kindly to film-makers tampering with the sacred text.

Caine was cast as Nicholas Urfe, an Englishman who arrives on the fictional Greek island of Phraxos to take up a teaching post. There he encounters Maurice Conchis, a Greek magician who uses his villa as a theatre where he stages complicated psychological charades to help visitors such as Urfe come to terms with themselves. Urfe's reality is continually being undercut – one minute Conchis is presenting himself as a psychiatrist, the next as a film director. Candice Bergen and Anna Karina, as mysterious female

Caine models a little off-the-shoulder number for the local Nazis in **The Magus**

interest, confuse the schoolteacher even further. In short, Conchis is a sort of magical mystical therapist, though one can't imagine he is doing Urfe any favours by encouraging him to think of himself as the centre of the universe, the man for whose exclusive benefit all the drama is being unfolded.

The critical view was that it might have worked, pretensions or no pretensions, if only the director, Guy Green, had cut loose with the surrealism. Instead it was dismissed as plodding and faintly risible, with Caine appearing miscast in a particularly thankless role. American critic Rex Reed declared, 'This may not be the most misguided movie ever made, but it's in there pitching.'

Conchis was played by Anthony Quinn, whose entourage began to give Caine the hump while they were on location in Majorca. Every day one of the older star's minions would forewarn the rest of the cast and crew as to whether the star was in a good or a bad mood. One day Caine responded with, 'Has he ever asked what mood I'm in?' and headed for the airport. They coaxed him back, but he had made his point: he was not going to stand for being treated like one of the grovelling lackeys. Caine and Quinn ended up the best of friends; six years later they would work together again on *The Marseille Contract*.

8

WAR MOVIES

By 1969 the image of Michael Caine had been indelibly stamped on the public consciousness. The elements of the 'package' he had deliberately set out to put together were all in place: he was the amenable working-class Cockney with the spectacles and cigar. 'It was the truth,' he said, 'but I had quite consciously assembled that truth so nobody could miss it.' Like the big studios in Hollywood's heyday, he had created a star image and then promoted it, only he had done it on his own behalf. And like the stars of that bygone era who had to play whatever roles their studio bosses ordered them to play, Caine worked non-stop, not waiting around for the role-in-a-lifetime to land in his lap, but accepting whatever came his way.

Towards the end of the Sixties, though, he began to express a few doubts. 'I'm tired of my image as a lovable Cockney,' he told one reporter. 'I'm a Cockney, certainly, but far from lovable. A lot of people probably hate the sight of me. So I'm making changes.'

Caine's changes weren't really changes at all. They included buying the most expensive Rolls-Royce he could find (even though he didn't have a driving licence) and moving to a flat in Mayfair, the most expensive square on the Monopoly board. 'It's very handy,' he said, sounding more than a little tongue-in-cheek. 'My tailor is just around the corner, there are plenty of shops, and it's just a brisk walk to Sotheby's, should one run out of antique furniture and need a quick Louis Quinze commode.'

'I would never appear in a war film that made any young man feel like going out and joining the Army,' said Caine. 'That was part of the reason I played in *Play Dirty*.'

René Clément was to have directed *Play Dirty*, but things just didn't work out and after two weeks was replaced by the film's associate producer, André De Toth, who had not only been executive producer on *Billion Dollar Brain*, but also had a long and distinguished career in directing behind him. Born in Hungary, he had worked for Alexander Korda in Britain before going to Hollywood. He had only one eye, but he never let that hamper his visual sense, even though he was unable to appreciate the 3-D effects on his own *House of Wax* in 1953.

The weary face of war;
Play Dirty

Melvyn Bragg, who had not yet made a name for himself as a telly arts guru, co-wrote the screenplay of *Play Dirty,* which was a variation on *The Dirty Dozen* – ex-convicts assigned to sabotage Rommel's oil depot in North Africa during World War Two. Caine plays their leader, Captain Douglas, and the film has a downbeat ending when the group is betrayed and most of them are killed. (This was apparently based on a real wartime incident in which the British sent a team of Palestinian saboteurs to blow up some oil dumps, and then, having decided to preserve the dumps but unable to contact the saboteurs by radio, alerted the Germans so they would be shot.) The two survivors – Caine and his second-in-command, Nigel Davenport – advance on their own troops waving a white flag. Unfortunately, they are also wearing enemy uniform, so are promptly shot dead.

The film was originally to have been shot in Israel, but there were insurance difficulties, and the production ended up amongst the sand dunes at Almeria in Southern Spain. So convenient was Almeria for the making of spaghetti Westerns that seven other movies were being made there at the same time, including *Shalako,* starring Sean Connery and Brigitte Bardot – Nigel Davenport was impressed when he saw Caine chattering away to her in French.

But the popularity of the location had its drawbacks. The crew had to keep clearing up the hoof prints and horse excrement left in the trail of the Westerns, while the Western production teams had the *Play Dirty* tank tracks to contend with. The process was so frustrating for everyone involved that Caine afterwards had a clause inserted into all his contracts that he would never again have to film there.

Play Dirty delivered the goods in terms of tough action, but critical reception was muted – mostly, one suspects, because of the uncompromising violence and an absence of life-affirming sentiment. Reading reviews from that era one gets the impression that film critics thought war films should depict combat according to Queensbury Rules. Caine's experiences in Korea had taught him that war was not a game of cricket, with the players having time to give farewell speeches before they upped stumps and retired to the pavilion. Real war was more a case of, 'One minute someone was there, and the next minute they weren't.'

Those critics who hated *Play Dirty* probably felt more at home with *Battle of Britain,* which was packed with moral uplift, stiff upper lips and national pride, a complete contrast to *Play Dirty.*

Caine's presence was fleeting but significant; it signalled that he

'One minute someone was there and the next minute they weren't'; Caine in **Play Dirty**

was now considered a star worthy of inclusion in the sort of all-star line-up in which the actors are so eminent they have to be credited alphabetically. For the first time, Caine was sharing top-billing with the likes of Laurence Olivier, Trevor Howard, Ralph Richardson and Michael Redgrave.

Harry Saltzman was producer, but there was a concerted effort to keep the flavour of the film British. One potential American backer was turned down because the company wanted the story told from an American point of view. Nowadays, of course, this probably wouldn't make much difference; British film productions fall over themselves to include at least one major American character so they can improve their chances of securing an American distributor. In 1990, *Memphis Belle* was touted as a British production, produced and directed by Britons, even though the story it told was of an American bomber crew, and all the main roles were filled by American actors.

Caine plays what he describes as a cameo – 'always makes me think of knickers' – in the role of Squadron Leader Canfield, who takes an early bath only halfway through the film when his Spitfire explodes, though we have to take someone else's word for this; there are so many planes blowing up it's difficult to keep track. Up until this point, the role has consisted mostly of him sitting around in cockpits, saying 'Roger, here we go,' and 'Yellow Section, keep your eyes peeled,' in a suitably Squadron Leader sort of accent. For most of the time, the only features visible beneath the flying helmet and oxygen mask are those blue eyes, which are necessarily engaged in swivelling around, trying to spot the enemy fighter-planes which have a habit of appearing out of nowhere. All we see of his private life is that old standby of the airplane picture – the trusty black labrador, later to be glimpsed looking doggily mournful when his master's death is announced. There is neither time nor opportunity for the actor to invest his role with anything like depth, but then 'depth' comes a long way down the list of requirements for this sort of film, below such things as 'battle footage', 'big explosions', and 'enormous great cast list of famous names'.

Whether or not you enjoy *Battle of Britain* depends on whether you like watching footage of Spitfires and Messerschmitts being put through their paces, for there is some truly spectacular aerial photography here, not to mention all manner of pyrotechnics when the bombs are dropped and half of London goes up in flames. What is missing is emotional content; one feels more sympathy for the anonymous pilots whose planes are shot from beneath them than for the unfortunate bit-players who every so often are clumsily wheeled on in order to be even more clumsily killed or bereaved. But denouncing the film as mediocre *apart* from the flying sequences surely misses the point – the film virtually *consists* of flying sequences.

The ground-based material is little more than filler of varying degrees of banality. Olivier, as Chief Marshal Dowding, gets most of the showy stuff – if you can describe keeping his lip stiff as showy – and there is an enjoyable cameo from Hein Riess as Reichsmarschall Goering, whooping it up as he sees the waves of German bombers departing from occupied France, but throwing a spoilt tantrum when the ragged survivors come limping back. Kenneth More puts in a token appearance to remind us of *Reach for the Sky*,

Squadron Leader Caine between takes; **Battle of Britain**

and there are some unintentionally hilarious scenes between Christopher Plummer and Susannah York, as a married couple who are constantly squabbling over whether or not she should seek a posting nearer to her hubby.

In the end, Plummer is horribly injured after being trapped in a burning cockpit, but just as we are relishing this knotty human conundrum – *will* all their marital differences be instantly resolved? *will* she ditch everything and run to his side, and never mind the radical face rearrangement? or will she shrink back in disgust, vowing never to go near him again? – the Germans are routed and the film finishes with Churchill's 'Never have so many owed so much' speech, which it is rumoured was recorded by an impersonator anyway. So now we will never know whether Plummer and York lived happily ever after.

9

SWANKY MOTORS

The Italian Job was the Sixties continental caper movie reworked as an 'I'm Backing Britain' promotion. The screenplay was by Troy Kennedy Martin, creator of *Z Cars*, who in the Eighties would also write the TV conspiracy thriller *Edge of Darkness*. Caine chose the script of *The Italian Job* himself and helped raise finance for the project. The music, which kicks off with *On Days Like These*, an airy Euro-ballad sung by Matt Monro, was written by Quincy Jones, who shared Caine's birthday – 14 March 1933. 14 March (though in 1879) also happened to be the birthday of Albert Einstein.

Caine plays Charlie Croker, a smalltime crook who is no sooner out of jail than he is plotting the perfect heist. Noël Coward plays his partner in crime, Mr Bridger – a patriotic crime boss who is still behind bars but who continues operations as though he were living in a luxury hotel, with the governor, guards and other convicts catering to his every need. Caine inherits a scheme from a late associate (Rossano Brazzi, neatly disposed of before the credits have finished rolling) to lift four million dollars in gold bullion from a security van in the middle of Turin. In order to do this, he and his colleagues fix the central computer and cook up the mother of all traffic jams, enabling them to snaffle the booty and slip through the chaos in a trio of red, white and blue Mini Coopers. Back home, in prison, the other convicts hail the triumphant Mr Bridger with a rousing *England!* football chant.

Caine's suit-maker gets a name-check in the credits, and the film has a pleasant late-Sixties fashion feel to it; his 'bird', played by Maggie Blye, wears a mouth-watering brown leather mini-skirt and matching jacket, and Caine sets off a series of pale outfits with eye-catching black leather gloves. In the first half hour, there are appearances from a number of well-known British faces – Benny Hill as a computer genius with a weakness for large women, Irene Handl as his sister, Simon Dee as a camp tailor, John Le Mesurier as the prison governor. The rabble of Cockney crooks is introduced (they include Caine's brother, Stanley, and a young Robert Powell), and the film's British credentials are firmly established – Coward collects pictures of the Queen, and the crooks will make their getaway disguised as English football fans. From this point on, characterisation takes a back seat to the details of preparation and execution of the heist. Even Caine, who gets the lion's share of the lines, plays second fiddle to the film's main selling-point – which is cars.

Though it would be many years before its star passed his driving test, *The Italian Job* ranks with *Bullitt* and *The French Connection* as a seminal car chase movie. Its set-pieces have since been copied so often that it no longer looks the novelty it once was, but director Peter Collinson, whose most entertaining film this was by a long chalk, does a marvellous job of transposing *Tom and Jerry* cheekiness into motoring manoeuvres. At one point in the chase, the Minis back into parking spaces and lie doggo while their pursuers race past unawares. They zoom through shopping arcades, down church steps where a newly-wed couple is posing for photographs, through pedestrian subways, down sewers and across a weir over the River Po. This is not just driving, not even just superb stunt-work, it is choreography of the highest order, motorised Fred Astaires doing the car-ioca all around town. Italian policemen in Fiats hang on their tails, but the Italian cars can't match the souped-up British ones and fall by the wayside. It is a wonder that Fiat agreed to collaborate, but since nowadays most us would rather own a Fiat Uno than a Mini, I suppose they have the last laugh.

The Italian Job ends with a famous cliff-hanger which leaves the story dangling literally in mid-air. For the last leg of their getaway across the Alps, the crooks transfer their loot into a coach, but the driver has obviously not seen *The Wages of Fear* (in which Yves Montand gets so carried away at having earned lots of money, he crashes his truck) and gets careless. The coach ends up balanced over the edge of a sheer drop, with the men trapped inside by the weight of the gold, which they are unable to reach without sending both it and themselves plunging down the mountainside. Caine's last words are, 'Hang on a minute lads, I've got a great idea.'

There *were* some ideas too, at script stage, perhaps kept in reserve for a possible sequel: one was for the crooks to keep the engine running, adjusting the balance of the coach by using up its petrol supply; another was to have the gold plummet to the bottom of the mountain, where it would be stolen by the Mafia. But the unresolved cliff-hanger ending was a masterstroke; it satisfied ethical demands (thou shalt not steal) without rubbing everyone's noses in the moral of the story, and above all it was memorable and got itself talked about.

On the face of it, the film is no more than a pleasantly breezy heist movie with a heavily British bias, so much a product of its era that it is probably more enjoyable to watch now, with the benefit of hindsight, than when it was first released. But, beneath Douglas Slocombe's sunny photography and the lightweight comic surface, there are darker undertones. That the film is taking the angle that cars are more important than people, for example, can be gauged by the way it presents violence. Blink, and you'll miss a couple of guards being clobbered hard over the head during the raid on the security van. But when the British crooks are stopped on a mountain road by the Mafia, the subsequent destruction of an Aston Martin and two E-Type Jaguars (as a hint that their drivers should back off and go home) is presented at length and in teeth-grinding, metal-crunching detail. It is more painful for the viewer to watch – perhaps because the destruction is so obviously real – than any amount of special effects violence against anonymous bit-players. Or perhaps we have been brainwashed into thinking that material possessions – and swanky motors in particular – are more precious than the health and well-being of people whose names we don't know.

And *The Italian Job's* jingoistic front is double-edged, because its most impressive hardware is used to break the law, and its staunchest patriots are criminals. Nowadays, there is an added piquancy due to the behaviour of English football hooligans abroad. It is difficult to watch *The Italian Job* without reflecting that disguising oneself as an English football fan is perhaps not the best way in the world to avoid attracting the attention of the authorities, and in Turin of all places – home of Juventus football club, dozens of whose supporters were killed in 1985 when Liverpool fans ran riot at the European Cup Final.

And after the destruction of his Aston Martin, Caine warns the Mafia boss that any violence against his person will be countered by organised retaliation against the entire Italian population of Great Britain. Any such persecution on racial grounds is not a nice thought, and here one gets a fleeting mental flash of the windows of Jewish businesses being smashed in by the Nazis. The film carries on its jaunty way, but it has some decidedly uncomfortable baggage in the boot.

'Hang on a minute lads,
I've got a great idea';
The Italian Job

10

MORE WAR

The corrupt Marcos regime was undoubtedly a Bad Thing for the population of the Philippines. It was, however, a Good Thing for Hollywood war movies, providing exotic jungle locations which could stand in for Burma, Malaysia, Vietnam and assorted Pacific archipelagos. Nearby American bases could cough up the appropriate hardware, and, as Francis Ford Coppola discovered when he was shooting *Apocalypse Now,* no-one objected if you wanted to wipe out a few acres of palm trees by dumping 1,200 gallons of gasoline on them. 'There aren't too many places in the world you could do it,' Coppola admitted afterwards. 'They'd never let you in the United States; the environmentalists would kill you.'

War is Hell;
Too Late the Hero

But the dubious charms of the exotic locations and local bars wore thin for the cast and crew of *Too Late the Hero* (1970). The film took six months to shoot in temperatures hovering around the 120 degree Fahrenheit mark, making redundant the spray-on sweat services of the make-up department. It was the longest shoot Michael Caine had ever experienced. He described it as absolute purgatory, though it would perhaps be a slight exaggeration to say, as he did later, that the whole thing might as well have been shot in the tropical house at Kew Gardens. 'It was just all of us looking out from behind a load of palm leaves.'

The director was Robert Aldrich, who also co-wrote the story and screenplay. Aldrich was one of those tough guy film-makers, like Sam Peckinpah and Sam Fuller, who loaded their war movies with an extra helping of grit. Most serious-minded cinephiles reckon he went off the boil after his first movie, *Kiss Me Deadly* (Mickey Spillane meets the Manhattan Project) but he found his biggest audience in the Sixties with Bette Davis and Joan Crawford slugging it out in *Whatever Happened to Baby Jane?* and the convicts-turned-commando war movie *The Dirty Dozen.* His later films – especially his last, the exuberant female tag-wrestling road movie, *California Dolls* – are vastly underrated by straightlaced auteurists, who tend to be suspicious of anything which is so entertaining. For many years, the director had the rights to Paul Bowles's *The Sheltering Sky;* one would dearly like to have seen his version (preferably starring Peter Falk and Laurene Landon as Port and Kit Moresby) in place of the dull, reverent plod through the desert that Bernardo Bertolucci made of it. He might have sometimes erred on the side of boisterousness, but one thing is for certain, Robert Aldrich was incapable of making a boring film. *Too Late the Hero* grips from start to finish.

We are on an island in the Pacific during the Second World War, and the cast list reads like a roll call of British war movie actors: Ian Bannen, Harry Andrews, Denholm Elliott, Percy Herbert. Even Sam Kydd pops up for an extended cameo as a Colour Sergeant. For the benefit of American audiences, Henry Fonda puts in a brief appearance at the beginning of the story, and Cliff Robertson is introduced as the nominal hero, Lieutenant Lawson of the US Navy, who is ordered to accompany a British patrol on a sortie to destroy the Japanese radio transmitter on the other end of the island. 'It's a suicide mission!' one of the soldiers exclaims, just in case we were labouring under the misapprehension they were setting out on a shopping expedition up the Brompton Road.

While on location, Robertson learned he had won an Academy

Award for his performance in *Charly,* but – Oscar or no Oscar – once out in the jungle, the audience rapidly transfers its allegiance from the Lieutenant, who turns out to be dour, somewhat craven and totally lacking in charisma, to the stroppy, cynical medical orderly, played by Caine, who has all the best lines – at least, he makes them *sound* like the best lines. As a bloodcurdling yell signals that yet another patrol-member has been picked off in the undergrowth, he turns to his neighbour and says, 'I reckon that makes you a sergeant, Jock.' Later, one of the soldiers steps on a landmine. Hearing the explosion, Denholm Elliott, as the ineffectual Captain Hornsby, asks, 'Where the hell is he?' 'You might say he's all around here,' replies Caine, eyeing the dead man's remains. 'As a matter of fact, you might even say he's got us surrounded.'

Caine, in a natty beret topped off by a pom-pom, relishes his role as the bolshie Private Hearne, a salt-of-the-earth type who gets himself arrested for a typically Caine-ish outburst of subordination, and his sick jokes capture perfectly the weary cynicism of men fed up with being shot at and stuck in a hellhole away from home for far too long; perhaps this last emotion wasn't so difficult for him to portray. The patrol makes it to the transmitter and Captain Hornsby proves his mettle by destroying it, at the cost of his life, and no thanks at all to the American lieutenant, who bottles out.

The handful of survivors are pursued back through the jungle by the enemy, led by Ken Takakura, iconic star of more than a hundred Japanese gangster movies, but now more familiar to Western audiences for his roles in Sydney Pollack's *The Yakuza* (helping Robert Mitchum see off the oriental Mafia) and Ridley Scott's *Black Rain* (acting Michael Douglas off the screen as his buddy in the Osaka police department). Takakura hoists a couple of loudspeakers up into the trees and bombards the fleeing men with offers to spare their lives if they will surrender. Three of the survivors give themselves up, leaving only Caine and Robertson at liberty. Caine's immediate idea is to save his own neck by hiding out in the jungle, but the American lieutenant, in a belated fit of patriotism, persuades him to head for home in order to pass on vital information about some Japanese planes they have spotted. To get back to base, the two men have to run across a mile of open no-man's-land, in full view of the enemy. This makes for a nail-biting finale as they bob and weave, trying to dodge the Japanese bullets on the home stretch. Robertson dies; Caine makes it back in one piece, if somewhat out of breath.

Too Late the Hero sticks to one of the classic thriller formulas – take a small number of characters, isolate them in a dangerous

'I was always very aware that I was a pawn who didn't matter very much.'
Too Late the Hero

situation, and see if any of them can make it out of there alive. It works in the war film (*Cross of Iron* and *Southern Comfort* are two which spring to mind) and it works, as well, in the horror and science fiction genres – *Alien* and its sequel *Aliens* are two of the most obvious examples. Most of the critics consigned *Too Late the Hero* to the *Play Dirty* dustbin when it was released, some of them appearing to find the body-count excessive, some of them even scoffing at the way in which so many people got blown up, as though forgetting that one of the salient points about war is that an awful lot of people get killed quite pointlessly. No-one could accuse the film of being less than realistic in that respect.

Caine did emerge from the long shoot with one memorable souvenir, however; he was introduced to Minda Feliciano, a Philippines Airlines hostess and the daughter of a cabinet minister. She accompanied him when he returned to London, where they stayed together until the newspapers started making noises about marriage. When the pair broke up, nearly two years later, Minda sold her story to the *News of the World*.

11

THE LAST VALLEY

The Last Valley was set in 1641, the twenty-third year of the Thirty Years War – this was the ding-dong between Catholics and Protestants which followed the Reformation and ended up with the map of Europe redrawn and Germany split into three hundred different states. Caine played the Captain of a band of mercenaries which happens upon an idyllic valley untouched by the ravages of war. Omar Sharif, the resident sage, persuades them not to do all the usual soldierly things, like plundering the valley and torturing its inhabitants. Over the following winter, he and the Captain forge a respectful friendship, but the man of war is recalled to his sword-swinging duties. Mortally wounded in battle, he returns to the valley to die.

The film was written and directed by James Clavell, whose novel *King Rat* had been filmed by Bryan Forbes, and who had previously written screenplays for (among other things) *The Fly* and *The Great Escape*. He had also directed a ragbag of movies such as *To Sir With Love* (Sidney Poitier on teaching assignment in a rough East End school) and *Where's Jack?* (Tommy Steele as an 18th Century highwayman). Clavell would later make an even more profitable living writing thumping great historical-oriental blockbusters such as *Shogun* and *Tai-pan*, both destined to become megabudget television mini-series.

The Last Valley seems to have been a turning point in Caine's career. It was the first time he had earned over half a million dollars for a film, but, more important, he gave a performance of which he was particularly proud. 'One of the best performances I ever gave, as a matter of fact.' More than anything else he had played, it was a role that owed nothing to his roots. The Harrys and the Henrys, Alfie, Charlie Croker – even Lieutenant Bromhead – all had something of Michael Caine in them. But here he had to assume the personality of a man from another time and another place, leading a way of life which was completely alien to the actor. For his role as the Captain, he had listened to English dialect records and from them devised a Germanic accent which didn't call attention to itself, but which was demonstrably non-English. But it

Caine trying to look at home on horseback on his way into **The Last Valley**

wasn't just a matter of technique; he felt it was a film which had something important to say about war, religion and the meaning of life.

Films and Filming rated him Best Actor of 1970 for his performance, and Gavin Millar of the *Monthly Film Bulletin* called it 'a convincing portrait of an intellectual who is also a man of action' and 'a superb central performance'. But elsewhere, *The Last Valley* and Caine's performance in it fell on stony ground, something which the actor was never able to understand. Many of the critics, and most of the public, refused to accept him in this new guise. Caine's packaging of himself as the amenable Cockney with the spectacles and cigar had worked only too well. Nobody wanted to see him in fancy dress.

In 1971, he told a reporter from the *Sun,* 'I've no intention of working just for money. I won't do anything unless I'm passionate about it.' It seems likely that the critical and commercial failure of *The Last Valley,* a film he really cared about, helped him overcome such idealistic sentiments, because before ten years were out he would be appearing in such turkeys as *The Swarm, Ashanti* and *Beyond the Poseidon Adventure.*

It is tempting to wonder what course Caine's subsequent career might have taken had *The Last Valley* been a smash hit. Would he have been cast in a lot of similar heavy-duty costume roles? Typecast as an actor of many accents, like Laurence Olivier and Meryl Streep? Would he have been more selective about his films, encouraged to appear in only those which contained a meaningful message? Or perhaps the failure of *The Last Valley* was a blessing in disguise, because, though in future he would be playing many different characters with a variety of accents, he would always be recognisably Michael Caine. Caine's strength as a screen actor is not a matter of taking on different appearances or accents, like a chameleon, nor of obliterating his self beneath another personality, as Meryl Streep and Robert De Niro sometimes appear to do. But then, Streep and De Niro are not film-stars in the way Caine is. Caine is always Caine.

'Captain and Valley Girl'
Caine and Florinda
Bolkan in **The Last Valley**

12

THE THREE MICHAELS

The Seventies were a great decade for Hollywood, though not many people appear to think so even now, because the successes tended to be more artistic than financial. The unexpected popularity of alternative low-budget films such as *Easy Rider* and *Night of the Living Dead* in the late Sixties had thrown what was left of the big film studios into a tizzy. By the middle of the Seventies, everyone was trying to clamber aboard whatever was supposed to be the latest bandwagon – youth, the devil, nostalgia, the buddy movie – anything that had struck paydirt. In this artistic free-for-all, directors were given their heads in a way which would have been inconceivable in the surrounding decades. While Steven Spielberg and George Lucas were revolutionising the nature of the blockbuster, and while old hands such as Sam Peckinpah and John Huston were proving they were still capable of delivering the goods, Francis Ford Coppola, Martin Scorsese, Robert Altman, Terrence Malick, Alan J Pakula and others produced films so off-kilter and uncommercial-sounding they would never have been given the green light a few years later, once Hollywood had locked into its obsession with box-office to the exclusion of all new ideas.

Unfortunately, the Seventies were also the decade when the British Film Industry went into a tailspin from which it has never recovered. In the late Sixties the American film companies, panicked by shifts in the economy and the market, had begun to close down their London offices and withdraw their backing from British films. As the Seventies got underway, British film companies were caught with their pants down in mid-Atlantic; unsure of what a British film actually *was*, or even if such a thing existed, their response was to churn out television spin-offs (*On the Buses, Love Thy Neighbour, Are You Being Served?* – the gruesome list is endless) and lacklustre remakes (*The Thirty-Nine Steps, The Lady Vanishes*). The *Carry On* films continued to paddle their line of smutty innuendo, seemingly unaware it had been made redundant by the proliferation of explicit sex scenes in mainstream movies. Other British companies poured money into American films; this ploy appeared to pay dividends with the commercial and critical success of *The*

Taking the Mickey; Michael Caine as Mickey King and Mickey Rooney as Preston Gilbert in **Pulp**

Deer Hunter, but eventually came unstuck with expensive flops such as *Raise the Titanic!* and *Honky Tonk Freeway,* which left Lew Grade and EMI, respectively, high and dry.

Get Carter offers a taste of what might have been. It sticks to a tried and tested film formula, but updates it so it looks fresh and exciting. Despite American finance, it is uncompromisingly British in its location, its actors and its language, but it has a story with universal appeal. And it is helped no end by the presence of a proper film-star; an actor with the X factor, someone you can't take your eyes off, even when he's playing a complete bastard. Films such as *The Long Good Friday, Mona Lisa* and *Stormy Monday* have since walked similar cinematic territory, but none have been quite so perfectly conceived or executed.

Get Carter was the first and last Great British Genre Movie of the Seventies. *Performance,* co-directed by Donald Cammell and Nicolas Roeg, had got halfway there in 1968, but its first-half portrayal of gangsters in suits had given way to a trippy hippy second half in which Mick Jagger and James Fox turned in, dropped off and bottomed out, and the story spiralled off into Borgesian ramblings. Three years later, *Villain* – featuring Richard Burton as a homosexual, mother-loving, East End gang boss – tried to pull it off, but failed. *Get Carter* went all the way, and scored a bullseye. It blew wide open the illusion that criminals were the lovable rogues of Sixties heist movies – not nice-but-naughty boys like Charlie Croker and Mr Bridger in *The Italian Job,* but psychopathic killers and vicious thugs, like the Kray brothers. It was the signal, if any were needed, that the Sixties were well and truly over, and tough times lay ahead. The Seventies were a decade of intense pessimism, when film-goers realised they could no longer rely on a happy ending. Bad guys didn't always bite the dust, sometimes it was the good guys who hit it, but the main problem was that it wasn't always obvious who the good and bad guys *were.*

At the beginning of the Seventies, Michael Caine was faced with the task of trying to shake off his relentlessly Sixties image. Harry Palmer, Alfie – in the eyes of many, Michael Caine *was* The Sixties, inextricably associated with Swinging London and its deceptive connotations of classlessness. But Caine was no overnight sensation – he had made good only after ten hard years of bit-parts and walk-ons; those years in the galleys had given him a steely determination not to sink out of sight at the first sign of a change in the tide. Here he was, only a few years after he had hit his stride, and already he was pushing forty. One might have thought this a liability for an actor who had ridden the wave of youth culture, but Caine's relative maturity proved an advantage. Actors who had always appeared to be his contemporaries but who were in fact younger – Terence Stamp, James Fox, David Hemmings, Tom Courtenay – quietly faded from view as the new decade gathered momentum. Other actors who were roughly the same age as Caine either seemed to have trouble finding film roles that suited them, were seduced back to the theatre, or were nursing a mighty hangover after a decade of hell-raising. Alan Bates, Peter O'Toole, Albert Finney all kept low profiles.

Caine certainly had no trouble finding roles – he continued to make two or three films a year, and not all of them were turkeys. But even in the turkeys, he would be learning all the time, broadening his experience, practising his technique, establishing himself as a true professional who could always be relied upon to arrive on set at the appointed time and do what was required of him with good humour and no hint of movie-star tantrums. The Seventies were the real testing time for Caine, but he hit them at a gallop, and audiences hardly noticed him slipping into middle-age. From being a leading man, he was graduating into being a leading man who was also a fine character actor: an unbeatable combo which would allow him to turn his hand to just about any type of role on offer.

In *Get Carter*, Caine stomps all over the last vestiges of his cheeky-Cockney-chappie image. Mike Hodges, directing his first feature film after working in television, has fashioned what is essentially a spaghetti western set in the North of England, his own screenplay based on the book *Jack's Return Home* by Ted Lewis. Even Roy Budd's music has more than a twang of spaghetti composer Ennio Morricone. Caine plays a man-with-no-name, except that he does have a name after all – Jack Carter.

We know this is not going to be *The Sound of Music* as soon as the film opens with the exclamation, 'Bollock-naked with his socks still on!' The characters, a London crime boss and his henchmen, are goggling at a pornographic slideshow. Carter exchanges meaningful glances with his boss's girlfriend – played by the very wonderful Britt Ekland – and it is later confirmed they are having an affair. As the credits roll, Carter catches a train and travels north to find out who killed his brother Frank, and why. He travels about as far as he can go and still stay within the borders of England – to Newcastle, where there are no wide open prairies, but some impressively dour industrial landscapes, a multi-storey car-park and a slag-heap.

On the train journey, we see him reading *Farewell, My Lovely*, but it rapidly becomes clear that Jack Carter is no Philip Marlowe, nor

is he even a tenth as chivalrous as the lone samurai of Akira Kurasawa's Japanese western *Yojimbo*, the model for Sergio Leone's *A Fistful of Dollars*. Carter is not entirely unprincipled; he has his own unwavering system of ethics, but mostly this enables him to kill, without compassion or compunction, anyone foolish enough to get in his way, as well as anyone who looks as if he or she *might possibly* get in his way, not to mention anyone responsible for Frank's death. At first, his aim appears to be simple revenge for his brother's murder.

No sooner has Carter set foot in Newcastle than he pays a visit to the equivalent of the western's saloon – the local pub, where he orders a pint of bitter, clicks his fingers impatiently at the barman and adds in a menacing tone that he wants it in a *thin* glass. Later on in the film, Carter allows himself a brief grin when the pub is the setting for another time-honoured western convention, a cat fight between an enraged girlfriend and the tarty cabaret singer who has been eyeing up her man.

Jack doesn't waste much time grieving over his brother, and the only traces of human feeling he displays in the rest of the movie are directed towards Frank's teenage daughter, Doreen, to whom he gives money. (When she tells him she's working at Woolworth's, he replies, 'That must be interesting'.) Only later do we find out that Carter once had an affair with his sister-in-law, and that it is more than likely that Doreen is therefore *his* daughter. His desire for revenge stems less from brotherly love than from a sense that he has been trespassed against *personally* – how dare they kill *his* brother. And again, when he finds out that Doreen has been making blue movies (Frank too had found out and this was why he was killed), he doesn't seem particularly concerned about her welfare. Normal people would bring the social services in on the act, but Carter prefers to murder everyone involved. Macho codes all the way from *Rigoletto* to *The Godfather* dictate that the daughter is her father's property, and crimes of property are not directed against the property but against the owner. Revenge is never taken on behalf of the victim; it is always for the benefit of the revenger.

Carter is ruthless in his quest for the culprits, an implacable avenging angel in a black raincoat. And with the first eruptions of violence, it also becomes apparent that he is not just your average

Jack's back in a black mac; Caine in **Get Carter**

The showdown on the slag-heap; with Ian Hendry at the end of **Get Carter**

anti-hero, but a complete psychopath. At one point we see him sneaking into the grounds of a big house belonging to Cyril Kinnear, the local Mr Big – played with a seedy lisp by playwright John Osborne ('Pith off, Ray' he says to a minion at one point). Carter clobbers a guard with skull fracturing force. Later, he stabs a man, throws another from the nineteenth floor of a multi-storey car-park, locks a prostitute in the boot of her Alpha Sunbeam and calmly watches as the villains push it into the river. He kills another prostitute with an overdose of heroin in order to get Kinnear arrested. Lest one should be tempted to let Carter off the hook by saying he is only violent towards other lowlife sleazeballs like himself, perhaps we should also remember the unfortunate driver who happens to be in the wrong place at the wrong time – when the man from the nineteenth floor hits the ground. Even Carter's allies get short shrift; he dismisses a helpful acquaintance who has got badly roughed up with a distinct lack of sympathy and a brusque, 'Get yourself a course in karate.'

Carter finds out that the man who poured whisky down his brother's throat and pushed him and his car into the river was Kinnear's slimy chauffeur, Eric Paice (played by the excellent Ian

Hendry). The final showdown takes place on a deserted beach which is more slag-heap than seaside. Carter force-feeds Paice on whisky and beats him to death with a shotgun. His quest, his reason for living, and therefore his life are now over; his vague plans to emigrate have always been the equivalent of the *film noir* character's impossible dream of escaping over the Mexico border. If Carter returns to London, the odds are he will be killed by his boss, who has found out about the affair with Britt Ekland, but he doesn't even get that far. Kinnear has previously hired a sniper, who now gets Carter in his sights and shoots him dead. End of film. The assassin, one imagines, is a man very much like Jack Carter; he even wears a 'J' signet ring. Or perhaps the 'J' stands for Jacobean Revenge Tragedy, a great build-up of corpses and nobody left standing at the final curtain. Violence breeds violence, revenge is a serpent which ends up swallowing its own tail, and nobody gets out of here alive.

We are now far enough away from the early Seventies for the fashions of time to look interesting rather than ridiculous. The men sport sideburns and wide lapels, the women wear bum-hugging mini-skirts, false eyelashes, and corkscrew ringlets, and the sleazy, pre-designer clothes suit the subject-matter down to the ground. As with *The Ipcress File,* what might have seemed like documentary realism now looks more like dirty surrealism. Hodges has a sharp eye for location and incidental detail such as the musical drinks trolley, the dollybirds who dance around their handbags at the disco, the partygoer who throws up in the goldfish pond, and the old biddies who witter on in the post-office about the man who has fallen out of the multi-storey car-park ('Really? Was 'e dead?' 'Ooh, yes.').

Another useful feature of *Get Carter*'s age is that the language now sounds surprisingly mild to ears accustomed to Eddie Murphy's non-stop cussing and contemporary films in which the word 'motherfucker' is considered *le dernier cri* in rapier wit. Hodges' screenplay is forced to rely on more colourful forms of address. In one memorable exchange, Carter describes Paice's eyes as looking like 'pissholes in the snow', and later calls Kinnear a 'hairy-faced git'. Despite the bleakness of the story and the nastiness of the characters, there is a great deal of graveyard humour. When Carter meets the chauffeur at the races, he says he is visiting relatives. 'Oh,' says Paice, 'that's nice.' 'It would be,' says Carter, 'if they were still living.' And later, when his landlady points out a small package that has been delivered to his digs, she asks him what is inside. 'My brother Frank,' replies Carter. These quips are a world

away from the sort of groan-making puns in the latterday James Bond films, or the ones made by Arnold Schwarzenegger in films such as *Total Recall* after he has dispatched his adversaries in various horrible ways. In Schwarzenegger's case, they serve to make him appear witty and loveable. Carter's comments simply emphasise his cold-heartedness.

As the film's publicity had it, Caine *is* Carter. Those hooded cobra eyes, used to such seductive effect in *Alfie,* come into their own here – his gaze is like ice, except when he catches sight of a young mother and her children, when it momentarily mists over with sentimentality. Jack Carter, one imagines, would have been as fond of his own mother as the Kray twins were of theirs; in his world, women are either madonnas or whores.

It was the first time Caine had played a character with no redeeming features whatsoever, a task that many actors, and most film-stars, would find daunting and dangerous for their public image, but Caine brings it off triumphantly, so triumphantly, in fact, that we never stop to question why someone who supposedly grew up in Newcastle should have a London accent instead of a Geordie one. Carter is an appalling character, but we stick with him all the way. *Get Carter* is a trip through a netherworld and he is our only guide.

Mike Hodges has said that when he first saw *Get Carter* on the big screen, he was stunned by its violence. 'It made me want to make a film about why people want to go and see violence, and about the commercialisation of violence. I wanted to make it funny, too. That's how *Pulp* came about.'

For *Pulp,* Caine teamed up for a second time with writer/director Hodges and his producer Michael Klinger. The film is a different kettle of fish altogether from the team's last collaboration; its critical reception was mixed, and it never received the distribution it deserved, but it now stands as one of the most original and entertaining films to come out of Britain in the Seventies. Some critics compared it unfavourably to the jokey John Huston film *Beat the Devil,* but it turns out to be a lot more disciplined than it at first appears.

It also provided Caine with one of his best and funniest voice-overs as well as his silliest Seventies hair-do. He plays Chester Thomas King, better known as Mickey King, a pulp novelist whose pseudonyms include Guy Strange, Gary Rough, Les Behan, S Odomy, and whose output includes such titles as *My Gun is Long* and *The Organ Grinder.* King's pages are sprinkled with crunchy

A publicity clinch with Britt Ekland, from **Get Carter**

violence of the 'blood spattered everywhere like a burst water main' variety, but the writer is not entirely satisfied with his lot. 'The writer's life would be ideal,' he says, 'but for the writing.' His solution is to dictate into a tape recorder and then get the tapes transcribed by typists.

The setting is all-purpose Mediterranean, though the film was mostly shot in Malta. One day King is approached by Lionel Stander, playing the factotum and bodyguard of the retired Hollywood star, Preston Gilbert, played with irrepressible gusto by Mickey Rooney. Gilbert is a big fan of King's novels and wants him to ghost his autobiography. King takes the job, the film star is assassinated, and the writer realises that he has been fingered as the next target by persons unknown who believe, wrongly, that Gilbert has spilled the beans on a past scandal.

The bare bones of the plot could be straight from a classic Hollywood *film noir*, or one of its updates, such as *Chinatown* or *Cutter's Way* – a hero, who is more idealistic than he realises, stumbles upon a past cover-up by members of a social and political class so eminent he is powerless to do anything about it. Lizabeth Scott, the growly-voiced femme fatale who sold Humphrey Bogart down the river in *Dead Reckoning*, puts in a *noirish* icon-like appearance as the wife of a local mayoral candidate (King asks her, 'Do you like being the wife of a politician – kissing babies and all that?' to which she replies, 'I don't stop at babies').

But if the story itself is dark, encapsulating all the weary cynicism of the typical Seventies conspiracy movie, the manner of the telling is witty and light handed, packed with original details (Caine is forced to take a five-day package tour on a coach in order to meet a contact), offbeat characters (such as Dennis Price as an English tourist), film and literary references both high and low (Price and Caine bounce lines from Lewis Carroll's Lobster Quadrille off each other). Hodges pulls off the trick of never allowing the references to overbalance the film, and piles on the laughs while never losing sight of his basic, rather downbeat premise. 'I wanted to do something light,' he said, 'as a bookend to *Carter*, to get away from the blood lust.' Compared with *Get Carter*, *Pulp* does appear to be a soufflé, but it is a soufflé which has been laced with a strong dose of strychnine.

There is a running joke at the expense of Caine's inability to drive (Hodges had found him out during the filming of *Get Carter*); as soon as the actor goes anywhere near a car, it crashes. As with *Carter*, there is some sort of showdown on a deserted beach; near the end of the film, he ends up in the passenger seat of a truck being driven by a one-armed man; when the driver is shot in his one remaining arm, Caine takes over the wheel and makes a hash of it. Meanwhile, the voice-over is providing non-stop patter – 'An ugly thought made my waters curdle' and occasional counterpoint to the action – King is shot in the leg and describes his heroic reaction in 'blood spattered everywhere like a burst water main' terms, whereas we can see that he has fainted clean away at the sight of a minor splodge.

With *Get Carter* and *Pulp,* it looked as if Hodges had found the ideal actor in Caine – a sort of cinematic amanuensis along the lines of John Ford and John Wayne, Sidney Pollack and Robert Redford, or Martin Scorsese and Robert De Niro. But the tribulations of working in the British film industry put the mockers on this enterprise. Hodges went to America to direct the engrossing Michael Crichton thriller *The Terminal Man,* starring George Segal as a scientist with mood-altering computers implanted into his brain. He followed this up with the hugely diverting *Flash Gordon,* marked time with the universally panned *Morons From Outer Space,* became embroiled in controversy when the IRA thriller *A Prayer for the Dying* was recut without his permission, and again demonstrated that he is one of the most imaginative and interesting British film-makers around with *Black Rainbow,* a bizarre tale of the paranormal starring the deliciously flaky Rosanna Arquette as a medium. Perhaps one day he will make another film with Michael Caine.

13

SOGGY OATMEAL

Caine took on the role of Alan Breck in *Kidnapped,* he said, because he wanted to appear in a film that his fourteen-year-old daughter Dominique would be able to see. It was his second appearance in a Robert Louis Stevenson adaptation (the first being *The Wrong Box*), though it was really two Stevensons in one since the film also incorporated the book's sequel, *Catriona.* The director was Delbert Mann, who in 1955 had won an Oscar for *Marty,* a cloying romance of homely folk, starring Ernest Borgnine as a Brooklyn butcher.

Kidnapped is held together by Caine's performance as the Jacobite rebel, rogue and daredevil, though a few critics were bemused by his Scots accent – at least one of them pointed out that 'loch' was pronounced 'lock' throughout.

But it was a troubled production which ran out of money halfway through, limping to the finishing line only with a great deal of difficulty. Caine didn't get paid his full whack and he never forgot it; as a thorough professional, he wasn't about to discuss the subject, but he must have been riled about being let down by the unprofessionalism of others.

By the early Seventies, his professionalism as a film actor was well known, but he learned a further lesson on location on the Isle of Mull, when the director announced an unexpected change of plan. The weather was so perfect Mann decided he wanted to shoot Caine's big speech that same afternoon, way ahead of schedule. It was a two-page soliloquy in which Alan Breck rhapsodises about his beloved Scotland, and the actor hadn't learnt a single word of it. But he requested an hour's grace, swotted like mad, and then delivered the speech in one take. The experience taught him something which he would later pass on: 'Learn your lines for the whole film before you start shooting.'

Married love; Caine with Elizabeth Taylor in **Zee and Co**

One film critic pointed out there was an awful lot of porridge-eating in *Kidnapped.* The breakfast cereal motif soon cropped up again in Caine's career. On a TV chat show in America, film critic Rex Reed commented, 'I can't stand the thought of our Elizabeth

Taylor being in love with you in *X, Y and Zee.* You look like soggy oatmeal.'

Caine replied, 'Well, that's better than looking like sugar-coated cornflakes.'

X, Y and Zee was the American title for *Zee and Co,* a daft drama of adultery with a screenplay by Edna O'Brien, who furiously denounced the finished film because the director, Brian Hutton, had tampered with her script, having had the temerity to rewrite or remove some of her scenes. 'If I meet him again I shall kill him,' she said in a television interview. Since it is not exactly unusual for screenplays to be altered in the course of production, it just goes to prove how little O'Brien knew about the film business and films in general. There might even be something to be said for the argument that Hutton didn't change the screenplay nearly *enough.*

Caine played Robert Blakeley, a successful architect and the first of his Seventies 'husband' roles. In the Sixties, he had mostly played bachelors; now he was considered mature enough to sustain a relationship on screen, though one would be hard-pressed to find much evidence of maturity in this particular screen couple. Blakeley and his wife Zee, played by Taylor in a series of unflattering tent-like garments, maintain a marriage fuelled by each other's petty jealousies and infidelities until calm, compliant Susannah York arrives to form the third point of the triangle. This time, it looks like The Real Thing, and Blakeley resolves to leave his wife for her. Zee fights back by throwing tantrums (a Taylor speciality), attempts suicide by slashing her wrists and ultimately trumps her husband by discovering that York was expelled from school for having an affair with a nun. Caine comes home to find both women in bed together.

After initial nervousness on both sides, Caine got on well with Taylor, though he regarded the constant furore of publicity which surrounded her as a Bad Thing. Too much gossip about an actor's private life can distract from the performance, and Caine wasn't keen on anything distracting from his. He has always had an ability to play the publicity machine *just enough* but not *too much;* just enough to project the image of a recognisable movie-star, but not so much that the audience will be thinking about his private life instead of the story whenever he is on screen.

But round about the time he was filming *Zee and Co,* Caine's eligible status was letting him in for rather too much press coverage and speculation. The girl-happy bachelorhood which had launched a hundred newspaper and magazine articles was fine for a young actor employed in swinging *Alfie*-type roles, but for a film-star who

Bonny Scotland; Caine and Vivien Heilbron in **Kidnapped**

would soon be in his forties, it would have ended up looking a little grotesque. No doubt it was his hormones yelling at him to stop playing the field and settle down, rather than some cold-blooded career move, but his nest-building instincts and desire for a secure emotional base were now in full cry.

In 1971, he bought an 18th Century converted mill house by the Thames near Windsor, and commuted between Berkshire and the flat in Grosvenor Square. The house provided him with his own tennis court, swimming-pool, sauna and trout stream. He took up gardening, which he always maintained was excellent therapy and cut out the need for psychoanalysis. And one night he was watching television when he saw a commercial for Maxwell House coffee.

The thoughts of most single, heterosexual men turn to marriage as they approach the age of forty, and Caine's were no exception. He was drinking a bottle of vodka a day and his weight had gone up to about fifteen stone. Because the ad was banging on about 'Brazilian beans', he at first assumed the woman in it was Brazilian and therefore out of reach – a rather naïve assumption for an actor who was so well versed in the tricks of the screen trade. But she was based in London, and he ran into someone who gave him her telephone number. Shakira Baksh, who had been born in British Guyana of Indian parents, had worked as a librarian before being crowned Miss Guyana and coming third in the Miss World contest.

They lived together for over a year before getting married on a trip to Las Vegas. Not long afterwards Shakira gave birth to a daughter, Natasha. 'When I met Shakira,' said Caine, 'I knew my days of running around were over.'

14

LOTS OF PLOT

Sleuth may not be the best film ever made, but 1972 was a milestone in Michael Caine's career, because in it he was playing opposite Laurence Olivier, the most celebrated British stage actor of the 20th Century. In the eyes of many of the critics, incapable of seeing that Caine was already a better screen actor than Olivier could ever hope to be, it gave him credibility as a performer. Caine's view was that with Olivier, he couldn't lose. 'If I am not as good as he is – and he is the best actor in the world – that won't be news, so no-one will be surprised. If I do give him a run for his money – and I will – people will say, "Fancy Michael Caine being able to do that", so I'll come off well either way.'

Sleuth was an adaptation of the successful stage play by Anthony Shaffer, and is a triumph of plot over content. For that reason, anyone who doesn't know what happens and is still busting a gut to see it should skip the next half-dozen paragraphs, as *vital twists* in the plot *are about to be revealed*. On the other hand, why not read all about it, and then watch a proper film like *Get Carter* or *The Man Who Would Be King* instead?

Plots are funny things – there aren't many films which can get away without having one, but once the backbone is there and the rest of the film clicks into place around it, it should automatically become one of the least important elements. Prior knowledge of what is going to happen shouldn't spoil your appreciation of a film; you can watch *Casablanca* or *The Seven Samurai* or *Chinatown* again and again, and it doesn't matter that you already know whether or not Ingrid Bergman lives happily ever after with Humphrey Bogart, or whether or not Toshiro Mifune lives to fight another day, or whether or not Jack Nicholson will make it to the Mexican border with Faye Dunaway. But *Sleuth* is one of those movies which, once you are acquainted with the twists and denouement, becomes an academic exercise – a brace of megastar turns pickled in plot devices.

The director was Joseph L Mankiewicz, fondly remembered for *All About Eve* and *Guys and Dolls,* though perhaps not quite so fondly remembered for the lumbering Taylor/Burton *Cleopatra. Sleuth* takes place almost entirely on one interior set, with a few exterior shots thrown in to prove that yes, we're making a *film,* and here's some sky and greenery to prove it. Olivier plays Andrew Wyke, a successful thriller writer, collector of junk and inveterate games player. Caine plays Milo Tindle, an upstart hairdresser who is having an affair with Wyke's wife Marguerite. In Act One (the film divides very easily into theatrical acts) Wyke invites Tindle to his country mansion and proposes Red Herring Number One – Tindle will break into the house dressed as a clown and steal Marguerite's jewellery so he will be able to keep her in the style to which she is accustomed; Wyke will collect the insurance.

But this is all an elaborate ruse to get to Sadistic Wheeze Number One: Wyke announces he will now shoot Tindle dead and explain to the police that it was self-defence. In fact, as we later find out, this is Vital Twist Number One: the gun has been loaded with blanks. Tindle, however, doesn't know it and makes a complete fool of himself, snivelling and begging for mercy. Caine, for once in fear of his life rather than putting other people in fear of theirs, lets himself go to pieces; his customary underplaying is replaced by hysterical blubbing, which is not pretty. Instead of sticking to his normal nerve-calming routine before shooting the scene, he had purposely let his nerves take over. 'I was surprised at the extent of them,' he said. 'It was relatively simple to become a gibbering wreck.'

In Act Two, Wyke is visited by Detective Inspector Doppler of the Wiltshire County Constabulary, who is investigating Tindle's disappearance and refuses to believe Wyke's claim that he did not murder him. Vital Twist Number Two: the play is a two-hander, and the other names in the credits are Red Herring Number Two; we are informed that Marguerite, for example, is played by 'Margo Channing' (the name of the Bette Davis character in *All About Eve*) even though her only appearance is in a portrait, and Doppler is down as being played by 'Alec Cawthorne'. Unfortunately, it is obvious from the Detective Inspector's very first entrance that he is not a third character at all, but Tindle in disguise, executing Sadistic Wheeze Number Two. In other words, it is Michael Caine in heavy theatrical make-up – receding hairline and a moustache, looking as if he's trying to pass himself off as Sean Connery.

This sort of wig-and-pate trickery might have worked on the stage, but on the screen it looks incompetent. On the other hand, one has to assume it was intentional, since it would have been so easy to kit out Caine with a more effective disguise. (You need look no further than *The Man Who Would be King*, in which he is almost unrecognisable as a mouldy old Indian beggar.) Suspension of

The greatest British stage actor of the 20th Century versus upstart movie star; Caine with Laurence Olivier in **Sleuth**

disbelief immediately flies out of the window. If *we* can see it's Tindle, why can't Wyke? Is the man blind? Our brains start working overtime. Aha, we think, perhaps he *has* recognised Tindle, but is pretending not to in order to spring another Sadistic Wheeze. But no; we have fallen prey to the film's plot-itis, and now we are seeing narrative twists where no narrative twists exist.

After tormenting Wyke for a while, Tindle whips all the rubber bits off his face and reveals his true identity. In the Third and Final Act, he announces Sadistic Wheeze Number Three: he has strangled Wyke's mistress and planted incriminating evidence around the house. Unless Wyke wants to be arrested for her murder, he will have to solve a number of jumped-up crossword clues so he can find the evidence and dispose of it. Wyke duly rushes around solving the puzzles. In Vital Twist Number Three, or possibly Number Four, Tindle reveals Sadistic Wheeze Number Four (or was it Three?) was a sham – he hasn't strangled the woman after all. Wyke, who can't bear the thought of being out-wheezed, does a replay of Sadistic Wheeze Number One, only this time the gun is loaded with real bullets. Since both characters are not more than pawns in Shaffer's Grand Theatrical Joke, nobody cares much either way. A real police car rolls up just as the final curtain is rung down.

If there is pleasure to be had from *Sleuth,* it lies in watching Olivier and Caine hamming it up, and though both have hammed it up more enjoyably elsewhere, their respective positions are at least summed up quite neatly by their roles. Olivier, as the lordly, successful writer locked in combat with the *nouveau riche* hairdresser, is also the established, patrician stage actor being challenged by the movie-star from a working-class background. Each role is chock-full of long emotional speeches and other showy business – they are forever breaking into funny accents, brain-teasing wordplay, silly walks, and snatches of song (Tindle is half-Italian, so Caine gets to do a blast of *Pagliacci*). Caine more than holds his own, but in truth, he is not furthering his film career so much as demonstrating that he can deliver a typically barnstorming theatrical performance with the best of them. For the consummate film actor, *Sleuth* is not cinema but vicarious theatre.

But Caine knew which side his bread was buttered on. He had had enough of theatre a long time ago. 'I associate the stage with misery, struggle, hardship and no money,' he said. 'But motion pictures have meant riches and delirious happiness.' And he advised Olivier to supplement his income with a few more film roles. Olivier went out and made *The Betsy*, *The Jazz Singer* and *Clash of the Titans* . . .

Both Caine and Olivier were nominated for an Oscar, along with Marlon Brando for *The Godfather,* Peter O'Toole for *The Ruling Class* and Paul Winfield for *Sounder.* This was the year that Brando won, and stunned the Academy by sending in his place Sacheen Littlefeather of the Native American Affirmative Committee to deliver a short speech about the film industry's mistreatment of the American Indians. Caine said afterwards he thought if Brando had wanted to make a gesture, he should have delivered the speech himself instead of letting Littlefeather face the music.

15

THREE THRILLERS

Caine made three thrillers on the trot in the mid-Seventies. The first and best of them was *The Black Windmill,* directed by the veteran Don Siegel, who had graduated from making superior B-movies in the Forties and Fifties (*The Big Steal, Riot in Cell Block 11, Invasion of the Body Snatchers*) to making superior B-movies on A-movie budgets in the Sixties and Seventies (including several Clint Eastwood vehicles, the best-known of which was *Dirty Harry*).

In *The Black Windmill,* Caine plays MI6 operative Major John Tarrant, whose son is kidnapped by members of the gun-running syndicate he has being trying to infiltrate. Donald Pleasance, as Tarrant's boss, suspects his employee of double-dealing and so refuses to pay the ransom of half a million pounds in uncut diamonds. Tarrant is forced to steal the diamonds and goes on the run to France, only to find himself framed for murder and pursued both by criminals and police. Eventually, he returns to England and with the help of his estranged wife (played by Janet Suzman), he rescues his son from the black windmill of the title, kills the bad guys and exposes the traitorous government official who had him framed.

The Black Windmill arrived too late to exploit the Sixties vogue for secret agents, but too early to cash in on the Eighties mania for moles-in-high-places which was to hit new heights of official paranoia with the publication of *Spycatcher.* The plot was complicated, full of double-crosses and false identities, and most of the critics were disappointed that Siegel had forsaken the violent America of *Dirty Harry* for the more genteel, less explosive terrain of British espionage. Caine too, though he had been eager to work with the director, thought the English location had rubbed away some of the rough edges which gave Siegel's work its characteristic drive. Yet *The Black Windmill* is not without its pleasures; it is a diverting shaggy-dog variation on Siegel's favourite theme of One Man Against the Rest of the World, and casts a wry outsider's eye on the convoluted goings-on in the ranks of British intelligence.

One man against the rest of the world; Caine as Major John Tarrant in **The Black Windmill**

Caine agreed to appear in *The Marseille Contract* (known in the USA

as *The Destructors*), before seeing a word of the screenplay. The locations undoubtedly helped; from the depths of a freezing British winter, filming in the South of France must have seemed like an irresistible prospect. 'I don't care what the script is like,' he said. 'I'll do it.'

Mind the doors; Caine goes underground in **The Black Windmill**

He was cast as John Deray, a professional hitman hired by Steve Ventura, head of the Parisian arm of the American Narcotics Bureau, to assassinate drug baron Jacques Brizard. Caine's old pal from *The Magus,* Anthony Quinn, was cast as Ventura. Brizard was played by James Mason, one of the few British screen actors capable of giving Caine a run for his money and, like Caine, always worth watching, even in inferior material. The relationship between Ventura and Deray, who turn out to be old buddies now working on opposite sides of the law, at first promises to add zest to the story, but it winds down into a routine ambush and shoot-out, in the course of which Deray is killed. Ventura is then left to bend the law by killing Brizard. The critics decided it was all disappointingly hackneyed, bearing all the hallmarks of an Anglo-French co-production with an illustrious international cast (Maurice Ronet held up the French end as a treacherous cop) fighting to make a silk purse out of a mediocre screenplay.

The third of this thrill-packed trio was *The Wilby Conspiracy,* a mis-matched-buddies-on-the-run movie set in South Africa, but filmed for obvious reasons in Kenya. The fact that one of the buddies is black and the other white automatically lends it a political dimension, though the film's politics are not exactly of the most sophisticated kind. The director was Ralph Nelson, whose *Soldier Blue* had antagonised liberal audiences by ramming home its humanist, pro-Red Indian message with what was thought to be an excessively splattery massacre scene.

PREVIOUS PAGE: ***Funeral in Berlin.*** *'Someone once said of Harry Palmer that he came on like a loser,' said Caine. 'I liked that – you could say the same of me.'*

'I only shout at bad actors,' said Otto Preminger, director of ***Hurry Sundown.*** *'I would never shout at Alfie.'*

RIGHT: 'I wanted to do something light,' said director Mike Hodges of ***Pulp****, 'as a bookend to* ***Carter****, to get away from the blood lust.'*

*For the consummate film actor, **Sleuth** is not cinema but vicarious theatre.*

*LEFT: Even Caine, who gets the lion's share of the lines, plays second fiddle to **The Italian Job**'s main selling point – which is cars.*

*'Roger, here we go.' Caine as the ill-fated Squadron Leader Canfield in **Battle of Britain**.*

*LEFT: Before **Zulu**, Michael Caine was just another face in the crowd. After **Zulu**, he was a movie star in the ascendant.*

'There are people who are actually trying to kill us!' Michael Caine as Noel Holcroft in ***The Holcroft Covenant****.*

RIGHT: 'I'm very well paid and I'm not worried.' Michael Caine after the critics panned ***The Island****.*

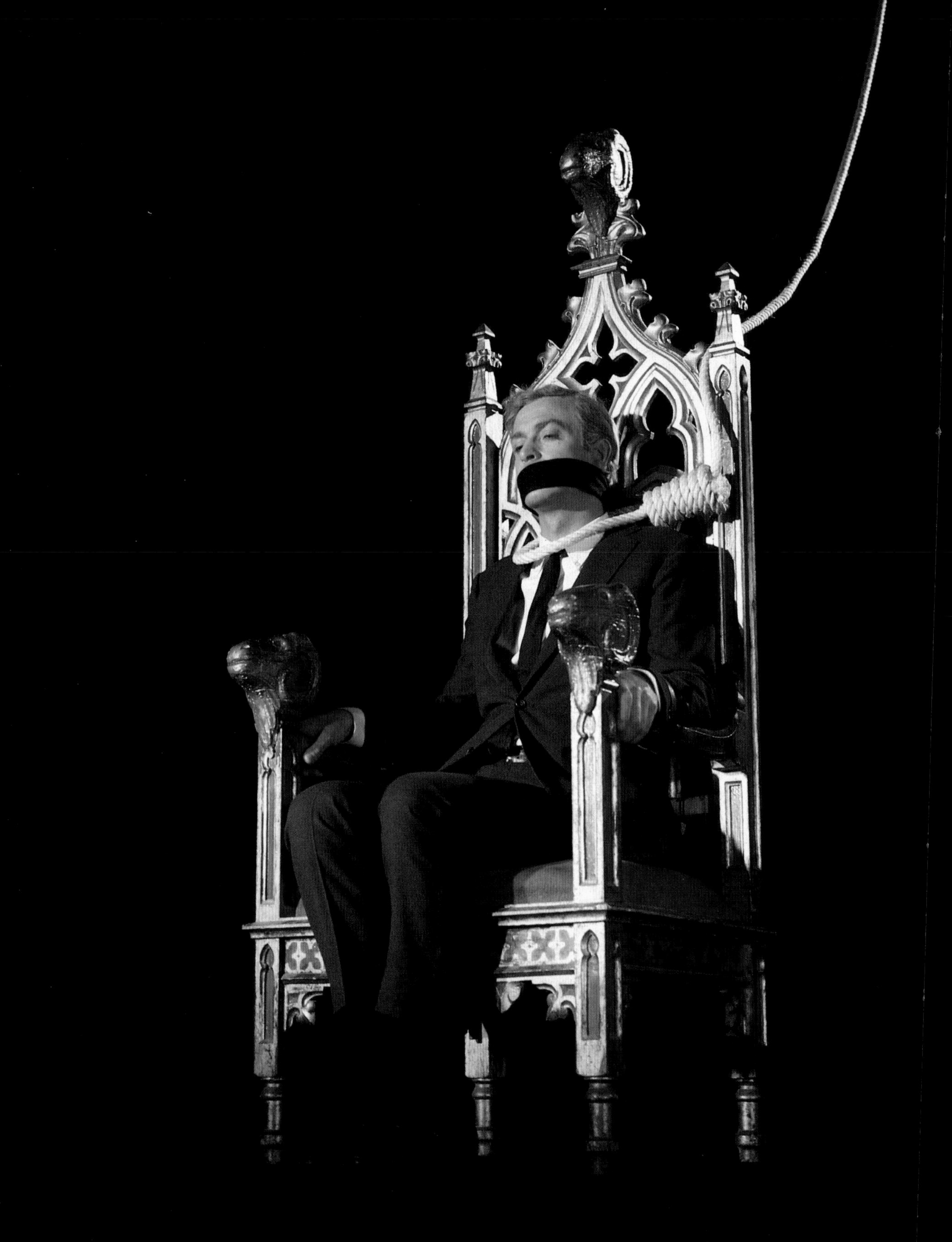

The Hand. *Sometimes, by accident, horror films have a habit of reaching the parts that other films dare not reach.*

LEFT: 'This may not be the most misguided movie ever made, but it's in there pitching' – Rex Reed on ***The Magus****.*

Blame it on Rio. *'I did it in order to prove that I could do comedy.'*

LEFT: Flying the Flag; Caine and scene-stealers in ***Water****.*

LEFT: 'Of course I'm drunk – you don't really expect me to teach this stuff when I'm sober.' Caine's third Oscar nomination came for his performance as Dr Frank Bryant in ***Educating Rita****.*

Loadsamoney; Caine the conman in ***Dirty Rotten Scoundrels****.*

OVERLEAF: ***Gambit.*** *'First it was the Beatles and then it was miniskirts, and now see what the British have sent us in the flicks – a cockney lad who's sure to be just our cup of tea.'* New York Daily News.

Had *The Wilby Conspiracy* been made in the Eighties, it would have slotted more or less into the cycle of films such as *Cry Freedom, A World Apart,* and *A Dry White Season,* well-meaning movies which don't beat about the bush in proclaiming their anti-apartheid message. Common to all these films is the requisite white Fascist villain, a Nazi by any other name. It makes it easier on the audience if the bad guys are shown to be evil monsters rather than ordinary people with a vile streak of bigotry added on. In *The Wilby Conspiracy,* the Fascist is played by Nicol Williamson, who approaches his role with Rottweiler-like sensitivity. Caine plays Jim Keogh, an English mining engineer who forms an uneasy alliance with black revolutionary Shack Twala, played by Sidney Poitier, Hollywood's most famous and seemingly – for many years – only black actor. In the time-honoured mismatched-buddy tradition, these two go on the run together cross-country, passing through all the usual stages of mutual antagonism and grudging respect. (Poitier might well have experienced a feeling of *déjà vu;* he had already had this sort of relationship back in 1958 with Tony Curtis in *The Defiant Ones.*) Eventually, both men band together with some black villagers to sock it to the villain and his cohorts.

This was one role which Caine did not accept on account of the location, nor did he do it for the money. 'I did that part purely because of the anti-apartheid angle,' he said. He had witnessed big-scale racial prejudice in action back in 1966, while filming *Hurry Sundown* in Louisiana. Having been on the receiving end of prejudice himself – the sort of prejudice which underestimates anyone who doesn't speak with a Home Counties accent – he had no time for it, and dealt with questions about his marriage to Shakira in typically forthright manner. He hadn't married an Indian woman, he said, he had married a woman who happened to be an Indian. 'The colour difference never presented any problem.'

He would later put his money where his mouth was by playing a white man married to a black woman in *Ashanti;* the film itself might have turned out to be absolute tosh, but in this feature alone it challenged convention. Romance between characters of different racial origins is still considered a dodgy subject in Hollywood today. Eddie Murphy, for all his box-office clout, was only allowed to go as far as a chaste kiss with white leading lady Charlotte Lewis in *The Golden Child.* Even in the otherwise impeccably liberal *Dances with Wolves,* Kevin Costner ensured that he fixed himself up, not with a winsome Sioux maiden, but with a white woman who had been taken in by the Native Americans and raised as one of their own.

16

TWO TURKEYS

Even the critics seemed to realise that *The Romantic Englishwoman* (1975) is trash masquerading as art. This was despite credits which included a famous name from the theatre, Tom Stoppard, and a much lauded American director, Joseph Losey, fêted for his rather ponderous dissections on English class, *The Servant* and *Accident.* Losey's best film by far (though I am prepared to admit this is a minority opinion) was *Modesty Blaise,* starring Monica Vitti and Michael Caine's ex-flatmate, Terence Stamp, as spoof secret agents variously menaced by ultra-camp supervillain Dirk Bogarde and some impressive, oppressive pop art set design. One of the film's high-spots is when Stamp peels a layer of rubber off his back to reveal an inflatable seagull underneath.

The Romantic Englishwoman could have done with a good dose of inflatable seagull. It takes itself so seriously it is in danger of disappearing up its own fundament. In synopsis, it sounds almost like a parody of the British life of Hampstead adultery, though this one happens to be set mostly in Weybridge, Surrey. Michael Caine plays Lewis Fielding, a successful novelist who is the complete opposite of Mickey King in *Pulp*; one imagines his novels are all about adultery in Hampstead (or possibly Weybridge), and I would rather be stuck on a five-day coach-trip with *My Gun is Long* any day. Fielding is currently working on a screenplay, and his creative juices are stimulated, as it were, when he begins to suspect his dissatisfied wife, played by Glenda Jackson, of having had an affair with handsome, mysterious drugs courier Helmut Berger when she was on holiday in Baden Baden. Berger ends up moving in with the couple, and lots of nail-bitingly inconsequential things happen until Jackson runs off with Berger to the South of France. Caine drives after them (or *appears* to drive after them – it would be eight years before he passed his test) and brings her home. Berger is led away by some sinister men who look as if they're going to fit him up with a concrete overcoat, or worse.

For a short while, Berger's absurd rent-boy mannerisms look as though they might add some sorely needed zest to the proceedings, but Caine and Jackson play such a boring bourgeois twosome that

The femme fatale with a handful of private dick; Caine and Natalie Wood in **Peeper**

it is hard to summon any interest in what happens to them. Caine has a slam-bang drunken tirade in a restaurant, but the rest of his time is taken up with looking alternately suspicious and exasperated. At least the role was something of a departure after a run of action heroes, a sort of non-action non-hero. 'It attracted me because for the first time in my life I was playing someone who if I met him in real life I would not only dislike but even despise,' Caine said of the role. He also called Jackson 'the best film actress I ever worked with.' It is a pity the two of them didn't pool their talents under more auspicious circumstances.

Peeper, which started life as *Fat Chance,* was a lame private eye spoof set in Los Angeles in 1947. Caine plays the down-at-heel British investigator Leslie Tucker (as the name for a hero, this is not exactly in the same class as Sam Spade), who is hired to find someone's long-lost daughter and give her a suitcase full of money. He discovers the child was adopted by a wealthy woman, but each of her two grown-up daughters (one of them played by Natalie Wood) claims to be the missing woman. After a spot of blackmail, attempted kidnapping and murder, Tucker solves the mystery, but

The indiscreet charmlessness of the bourgeoisie; Caine sizes up Helmut Berger in **The Romantic Englishwoman**

gives the money to the wrong woman because he has fallen in love with her. Caine enjoyed working on the production, especially that part of the screenplay which required the characters to visit the Caribbean on a luxury liner, but admitted the result was a disaster. As the hinge for a plot, deciding which daughter to present with the loot, doesn't carry as much of a dramatic charge as a murdered partner or a Maltese Falcon. The fundamental problem is that spoofing the private eye film is spoofing a genre which is already loaded with its own brand of deadpan humour. *The Black Bird* , with George Segal as Sam Spade Jr, was another film which tried it that same year and fell flat on its beak.

But the biggest problem facing both *Peeper* and *The Black Bird* was their makers' refusal to acknowledge that the goalposts had moved. Both productions were foundering in the wake of two remarkable movies which had changed forever the shape of the private eye thriller as we knew it. Though both had comic moments, neither of them could be classified as comedy – both, in fact, inclined towards the tragic – but they seized on the conventions of the form, rattled them around and stood them on their heads, subverting audience expectations just as all the best comedies do. Robert Altman's *The Long Goodbye* (1973), with Elliot Gould as a man-out-of-time Philip Marlowe, demonstrated how to update the private detective to modern LA, inject dollops of humour and irony into the story without ever descending to the level of cheap parody, and *still* have change left over to reflect on life, the universe and everything. One year later, Roman Polanski's *Chinatown* pulled off a similar feat in period costume, with Jack Nicholson, as JJ Gittes, walking the mean streets of Los Angeles in the Thirties.

These were hard acts to follow, and *Peeper,* by aiming for superficial pastiche, doesn't even come close, which is a shame, because Caine is a past master at portraying that cynical world-weariness masking a naïve romanticism which is the hallmark of the private eye hero. In fact, *Peeper* is a redundant exercise, because Caine had already made a private eye movie it would be hard to beat, though he doesn't actually play a private eye in it. Mickey King, in *Pulp,* may be a novelist, but he is also the blood brother of Gould's Marlowe and Nicholson's Gittes – well-meaning men all at sea amongst the sharks.

17

ONE CLASSIC

John Huston first read Rudyard Kipling's short story, *The Man Who Would Be King*, when he was fourteen years old, and started toying with the idea of making a film of it in 1952. He worked on the screenplay with Peter Viertel (whose *roman à clef* about Huston, *White Hunter, Black Heart,* was filmed in 1990 by Clint Eastwood), and used the location-scouting expedition as an excuse to go hunting for a Bengal tiger.

Humphrey Bogart and Clark Gable were originally cast in the two central roles, but when Bogart died, the project was shelved. Some years later, while shooting *The Misfits,* Gable let Huston know he was still interested, but he died soon after filming was completed. Over the next few years, the names of Marlon Brando, Richard Burton and Peter O'Toole were all being bandied about, but for various reasons the project never got off the ground. But in 1969, the huge success of *Butch Cassidy and the Sundance Kid* ushered in the era of the male buddy movie, and *The Man Who Would Be King*

Peachy and Danny; Caine and Connery in **The Man Who Would Be King** once again became a bankable proposition.

In fact, by now there were three different scripts, and Huston wrote yet another one with Gladys Hill. *Butch Cassidy*'s producer, John Foreman, who had worked with Huston and Paul Newman on *The Life and Times of Judge Roy Bean* and *The Mackintosh Man*, suggested Newman for one of the roles, and Robert Redford was set to star opposite him in a reworking of their Butch and Sundance relationship. But though Newman thought the screenplay was one of the best he'd ever read, he came to the conclusion that he and Redford would be miscast as Victorian Englishmen. 'For Christ's sake, John,' he said to the director. 'Get Connery and Caine!' So Connery and Caine it was.

From John Huston's debut (*The Maltese Falcon*) to his swansong (*The Dead*), the director demonstrated he had an exceptional talent for adapting written fiction for the screen, respecting his source material just enough but not too much, and creating something a world away from the chintzy Brit-lit costume pics of the Eighties – respectable but mind-numbingly dull films such as *A Passage to India*, *A Handful of Dust* or *A Summer Story*. *The Man Who Would Be King* lifts much of its dialogue directly from the pages of Kipling, but the film is more than just animated text. It has a life of its own. It *fizzes*. And Huston's enthusiasm and affection for the story shine through. It is one of the finest films in which Caine has appeared.

Like all the best works of art and entertainment, it operates on many different levels. It is a study of the shortcomings of imperialism, a study of the abuse of power, a tragedy of men made blind to anything beyond short-term material acquisition. It treats its source material with respect, but avoids nostalgia for the days of the Raj by acknowledging the story as a prophetic parable of the Empire's decline. The scenery (Morocco standing in for the Northwest Frontier) is exquisite, the performances spot-on, the direction unobtrusive but effective in the service of the plot. But perhaps most important of all, it offers a rattling good yarn, as one might expect from something which takes a Kipling story as its source. It is also a buddy movie, which places it squarely in the Seventies, though the period costumes and production design (by, respectively, Edith Head and Alexander Trauner, both veterans in their fields) avoid the sort of inadvertent date-stamping apparent in other period productions of the time such as *The Sting* and *The Great Gatsby*. Warren Beatty's sideburns in the otherwise authentically dressed *McCabe and Mrs Miller* now look *very* Seventies, but Caine's sideburns in *The Man Who Would Be King* are impeccably Victorian mutton-chops.

Caine and Connery bound for Kafiristan in **The Man Who Would Be King**

Huston was well known for his hands-off approach to actors. He cast his films with the utmost care, maintaining that once the right performers had been chosen, the director should have enough confidence to let them get on with it, and no need for him to interfere. 'It's a marvellous role for me,' said Caine. 'Humour, a good change of pace, a real gift.'

Most of the narrative is in flashback. Christopher Plummer plays Kipling, and the story is told to him by Caine, doing another one of his voice-overs. This is one occasion on which he was able to play up his London accent for all it was worth, while Connery as usual makes not the slightest attempt to disguise his Scots.

Peachy Carnehan (Caine) and Danny Dravot (Connery) are a pair of disreputable ex-army sergeants who have chosen to stay on in India rather than return to England, where they would be forced to take the sort of lowly manual job befitting their humble origins. They are scoundrels, dabbling in blackmail, theft and gunrunning, but their friendship is firm and they have a taste for adventure, preferably adventure which will make them incredibly rich. To this end, disguised as a mad priest and his servant, they plan to undertake the hazardous journey through the Khyber Pass and over the Hindu Kush to distant Kafiristan, where they intend to set themselves up as kings. When they outline this scheme to a bemused Kipling (who has recognised them as fellow Masons) he informs them that if they survive the journey, they will be the first white men to set foot in this area since Alexander. 'Well,' says Peachy, who has had to have it explained to him who Alexander was. 'If a Greek can do it, we can do it.'

After trekking across rivers and over mountains, the two men reach Kafiristan and win over the populace with a combination of rifle-power and condescending benevolence, drilling the locals into the semblance of an army and frowning at such barbaric practices as playing polo with the severed heads of enemies. Everything goes according to plan until Danny is struck by an arrow. He survives without a scratch, and the natives, unaware he was protected by his ammunition belt, hail him as a god. His divine status seems assured when the High Priest mistakes the Masonic emblem he wears around his neck for the symbol of Alexander, and the two men are given access to a treasure trove of gold and precious stones.

'These here make the jewels in the Tower of London look like cheap family heirlooms,' says Peachy, intending to escape with some of the loot as soon as spring makes it possible to travel back across the mountains. But Danny's godly pose goes to his head, and he begins to babble about fulfilling his destiny as the Son of Alexander. When a god takes a mortal bride, according to legend, she will burst into flames, and when Danny insists on getting married, his bride bites him in terror. As soon as the natives see the blood, the jig is up. Danny is flung to his death in a canyon, while Peachy barely survives to dump his friend's crowned head on Kipling's desk as proof of the adventure.

Huston had originally cast fairhaired Tessa Dahl (daughter of Roald Dahl and Patricia Neal) in the role of Danny's bride, Roxanne, but at the eleventh hour decided the contrast with the dark-skinned Moroccan extras would have been too much for an audience to accept. So he persuaded Shakira Caine to step in and take the role. Shakira, whose only big screen appearance had been as exotic and decorative interest in *Carry On Again Doctor*, insisted she didn't know how to act, but she certainly looked the part and, in the event, her non-acting is perfect for the role. The most difficulty she had was in the wedding scene, when she is supposed to be overcome with terror; Huston solved the problem by getting her to roll her eyeballs, showing the whites of her eyes so that she appears almost rigid with fear.

Danny and Peachy regard Roxanne in the same way they regard everything native, as something that has no worth until it is Anglicised and transplanted into familiar surroundings. 'Give her a hat with an ostrich feather in it, and there'll be no girl in Brighton on bank holiday could hold a candle to her,' says Danny, blind to the possibility that she could be perceived as beautiful amidst the trappings of her own culture.

Though Connery gets the marginally showier role with the mad priest's dance, the gold crown and the fleeting nude scene as the holy robes are lowered over his head, Caine has at least one scene in beggar-man make-up (grime, scars, one sightless eye) so effective that one wonders why they couldn't have made a better job of his policeman disguise in *Sleuth*. Together, they are a superb double act, neither trying to upstage the other, but working for the good of the picture as a whole. 'This was the best relationship I've ever had with another actor,' said Caine. 'We gave to each other all the time. It made it much easier to become those characters.'

Huston would offer the occasional piece of invaluable advice, such as suggesting that, since Caine was playing a man who was fundamentally honest, he should speak more quickly. But mostly he let them get on with it. 'It was like watching a polished vaudeville act,' Huston wrote in his autobiography, 'everything on cue, and perfect timing.' After three days of shooting, he stopped calling them by their own names, and started calling them Danny and Peachy.

Unfortunately the production had a slightly bitter aftermath. Connery and Caine had worked for a flat fee plus a percentage of the gross. ('I'm only interested in a percentage of the gross,' Caine had said earlier on in his career, 'all those other percentages of profits and so on are nonsense.') In 1978, the actors took out a lawsuit against Allied Artists, one of the film's backers, claiming they had not received all the money due to them. An audit showed there were irregularities on the company's books. Connery gave an outspoken interview about the affair, and Allied Artists counter-sued, alleging the pair had hatched a scheme to damage the company through false and defamatory statements. The actors eventually won their case.

Connery, who in the mid-Seventies was averaging three lawsuits a year, is famously litigious. Caine is less so. Ironically, one of his rare court actions was over a role which ended up going to Connery: that of William of Baskerville in *The Name of the Rose* (1986). Caine said he had been offered one and a half million dollars, plus ten per cent of the gross, so long as he lost twenty pounds in weight before the start of principal photography. Unfortunately for him, it was decided that the Californian court where he took out the action had no jurisdiction over the film company, because it was based in France.

18

WAR REVISITED

With *The Eagle Has Landed*, Caine was back in Britain, shooting in locations only ten minutes away from his Berkshire home. The film was based on a Jack Higgins novel with a central premise vaguely similar to that of Frederick Forsyth's *The Day of the Jackal* (filmed in 1973 by Fred *High Noon* Zinnemann), which describes an attempt to assassinate De Gaulle during World War Two. In *Eagle*, the target is Winston Churchill, whom the Gestapo want kidnapped and brought to Berlin. In both cases, history has tipped the audience off as to the eventual outcome, so the films must stand or fall on the way in which their tales are told. *The Eagle Has Landed* can't match *The Day of the Jackal* in tension, but has enough gatta-gatta action and daft performances to give it sporadic zip. The director was John Sturges, veteran of straight-up action fodder such as *The Magnificent Seven* and *The Great Escape*.

Spot the biggest ham; Donald Sutherland and Robert Duvall with Caine (and cigar) in **The Eagle Has Landed**

Caine plays German officer Kurt Steiner, who assembles a crack-team of paratroopers to infiltrate a Norfolk village disguised as Polish soldiers. Unfortunately, the Germans keep their German uniforms on beneath their Polish disguise (presumably to avoid being shot as spies, though as all of them end up getting shot anyway, one wonders why they bothered). The plan goes off the rails when one of Steiner's men plunges into a millstream to save a local brat from a fate worse than chopped salami; he gets mangled in the wheel, and his German uniform is exposed to the gawping onlookers. Realising the gaff is blown, the Germans take the villagers hostage, and after a shoot-out with some passing Americans, Steiner emerges the sole German survivor. He abandons the kidnapping wheeze and, resorting to what must be Plan B, kills Churchill, only to be shot dead himself by the big man's rather lackadaisical bodyguards. But all is not what it seems. Steiner has succeeded only in killing a *Churchill impersonator,* though presumably not the one who recorded all those famous speeches for the BBC. But fate has another twist up its sleeve; it would seem that the Churchill impersonator's bodyguards have succeeded only in killing a *Steiner impersonator,* because Kurt Steiner turns out to be one of the main characters in Jack Higgins's 1991 sequel *The Eagle Has Flown.* Perhaps there will be another sequel, called *The Eagle Has Laid an Egg.*

Caine's performance as Steiner is in the muted action-man mould, clean-cut, decent, and, like the actor himself, rather partial to big cigars. Tom Mankiewicz's screenplay takes immense pains to convince us that yes, he's a German officer, but at least he's a *nice* German officer; in his first scene we see him losing his cool and striking an SS General for his brutality towards some Jewish prisoners. For this he gets a death sentence, but is reprieved in order to lead the Churchill-nabbing mission. He is 'intelligent, ruthless, a brilliant soldier, but above all a romantic fool', and he has been educated in England, which means he speaks the language perfectly. 'You have to play it like a German trying to speak perfect English,' said Caine, who had already taken this approach with the character he played in *The Last Valley.*

At times, Caine underplays it so successfully that one almost overlooks him, particularly when some of his fellow actors are hogging the screen with performances so ripe they're on the point of bursting. Robert Duvall, as German intelligence officer Max Radl – the man behind the plan – sports a show-stopping eye-patch *and* a black leather glove which appears to conceal a mechanical arm, putting one in mind of Lionel Atwill in *Son of Frankenstein.* Donald Pleasence delivers one of his enjoyable slimeballs-from-history numbers as Heinrich Himmler – almost on a par with his creepy Thomas Cromwell in *Henry VIII and His Six Wives.* Pleasence, incidentally, is one of the few actors who can make Michael Caine's workload seem light – in the five years leading up to *Eagle,* he appeared in twenty-six films.

Larry Hagman, later to achieve immortal status as *Dallas*'s JR, plays an American Colonel who rants and raves before being shot between the eyes. Most preposterous of all is Donald Sutherland as a lovable IRA terrorist. We know he is supposed to be lovable because he disapproves of blowing up innocent passers-by, and his allegiances are due to anti-Empire sentiments rather than anything more controversial and sectarian. Sutherland, assigned to help in the kidnap attempt, gets to speak in a loopy Oirish accent, and he is also saddled with the daftest bits of the plot. Though a trained assassin, no sooner has he landed in Norfolk than he loses his heart to local teenager Jenny Agutter and becomes embroiled in unseemly, attention-grabbing fisticuffs with a rival suitor. He also gets a job as a marsh-warden, and it is symptomatic of the film as a whole that the only marsh in the area appears to be actress Jean Marsh – an East Anglian resident who turns out to be spying for the Germans because she is still miffed about the outcome of the Boer War.

It is interesting to compare *The Eagle Has Landed* with another war film which was released at about the same time in 1977, and which also has a German called Steiner for its central character. Sam Peckinpah's *Cross of Iron,* starring James Coburn, is grim, moving and full of the moral shadings in which *Eagle* is so conspicuously lacking. It illustrates the difference between an uninspiring but mildly amusing potboiler made from a comic-book yarn and a grim, compelling examination of the nature of war made by a master film-maker. Caine, an actor quite capable of carrying either sort of film on his shoulders, happened to be in the wrong place at the wrong time and ended up in the wrong film.

A Bridge Too Far, Caine's next war film, could almost be rechristened *A Star Too Far,* or perhaps *Twelve Stars Too Many.* With its razzle-dazzle roster of stars, it was like *Battle of Britain* all over again, minus the stunning aerial photography, hilarious Susannah York-Christopher Plummer subplot, and triumphant Hun-bashing climax set to music by William Walton. The production of *A Bridge Too Far* must have required at least as much logistical planning as the World War Two military exercise it dramatised. It turned out to be almost as much of a disaster; the big difference being, of course, that this time it was only money that was at stake.

Most of that money came out of the pocket of Joseph E Levine, the man who had financed *Zulu.* Levine's story – like Caine's – was classic rags-to-riches stuff. He had grown up in the slums of Boston, quit school at fourteen, and worked as a clothier and travelling salesman before getting his first sniff of celluloid as the owner of an art house in New Haven, Connecticut. Eventually he moved into the distribution of foreign films such as *Bicycle Thieves* and *8½*, and thence into production; *The Graduate* and *The Lion in Winter* were his. In *Adventures in the Screen Trade,* William Goldman reports Levine's reckoning that *A Bridge Too Far* was the four hundred and ninety-second film he had either produced, co-produced, financed, presented or distributed.

Goldman, who wrote the screenplay, maintains that *Bridge* turned out to be a commercial, if not a critical, success but at the start of the Eighties it was still being listed amongst the Forty Major Flops of All Time. God only knows why Levine decided that Cornelius Ryan's bestseller would make a good movie. It can't have been a desire to make money which persuaded him; big-scale war films such as *Battle of Britain, Waterloo* and *Tora! Tora! Tora!* had all been box-office disasters. Perhaps it was the hopelessness of the enterprise which attracted him. And for hopeless enterprises, one need look no further than Great Britain, which is addicted to them.

The British share with that other insular people, the Japanese, a penchant for the nobility of failure. Many a celebrity – Michael Caine included – has bewailed the British tendency to belittle success, while incompetent amateurs such as ski-jumper Eddie the Eagle are elevated to the status of national heroes. The Charge of the Light Brigade was immortalised by Alfred Lord Tennyson; the Battle of Waterloo had to make do with Abba. It is hard, though, to imagine even British audiences wanting to pay good money to watch an Allied plan to seize six Dutch bridges going disastrously wrong thanks to inadequate planning, boneheaded obstinacy and sheer bad luck. German tank divisions pop up in places where they're not supposed to be, fog delays vital parachute drops, the RAF dumps vital supplies behind enemy lines. So where's the fun in that?

Even as experienced a screenwriter as Goldman found himself faced with an enormous number of creative obstacles. With such a broad canvas, what do you focus on? With so many stars, who gets precedence? Even with one hundred and seventy-five minutes running-time, Dirk Bogarde, James Caan, Michael Caine, Sean Connery, Edward Fox, Elliott Gould, Gene Hackman, Anthony Hopkins, Hardy Kruger, Laurence Olivier, Ryan O'Neal, Robert Redford, Maximilian Schell and Liv Ullman (listed in alphabetical order) will be allocated an average of twelve and a half minutes each, and that would be without taking into account all the requisite footage of planes, parachutes and exploding tanks. And then one has also to make room for Denholm Elliott as an RAF Met officer who has to deliver a long and characterful monologue about fog.

The chunkiest role goes to Hopkins, as the Lieutenant-Colonel leading the British battalion which gets stuck holding the Bridge at Arnhem without back-up. Redford, who probably got paid the most, is assigned the most gung-ho, over-the-top bit of heroics – charging across the Rhine in full view of the German troops. 'I need a man with very special qualities,' says Brigadier-General Ryan O'Neal, looking Redford in the eye. 'We're going to make the crossing by daylight.' Redford demonstrates he is a man of few words. 'Daylight,' he echoes in a meaningful monotone.

The award for the hammiest performance must go to Gene Hackman, playing a Polish Major-General with an ear-popping Polish accent which one suspects has been purposely designed to send the whole thing up. Hackman pronounces all his Gs hard, giving an interesting new slant to lines such as, 'General Browning, what of the Germans?'

Caine, by comparison, doesn't have to do much except brush up his uppercrust accent and wear his flashy green cravat with pride. He plays Lieutenant-Colonel J.O.E. Vandeleur, who heads a ground column of the British XXXth Corps into Eindhoven. It's another one of his officer roles, and most of it consists of him standing in tanks and jeeps, looking as if he's going somewhere. Not a lot was required of him as an actor, perhaps because the real J.O.E. Vandeleur was not only still alive, but also present on location as one of the production's military consultants, and you can't take too many liberties with the life of a man who is standing right in front of you. Caine's major creative input was replacing the scripted line, 'Forward, go charge', with what Vandeleur had actually said, which turned out to be, 'Well, get a move on, then'.

This is the sort of production which doesn't need a film director so much as a Field-Marshal; Richard Attenborough did the honours. With too many famous faces and no strong narrative hook, the film fractures into a series of unconnected episodes, and one is forced to delve into strange and tasteless territory to keep one's interest ticking over. Compare, for example, the many variations on the theme of *aaagh* as is uttered by stricken soldiers; the *aaagh* of being shot in the chest is very different from the *aaagh* of being dragged across the tarmac after having caught one's trouser-leg in the door of a jeep. In *A Bridge Too Far* there are many, many *aaaghs*.

19

TAX

Harry and Walter Go To New York was in the mould of the box-office smash *The Sting* – a period film which is also a caper film which is also a buddy movie. *The Sting,* though, had the *Butch Cassidy and the Sundance Kid* dream ticket of Paul Newman and Robert Redford. *Harry and Walter,* set in 1892, had to fall back on James Caan and Elliot Gould as vaudeville performers turned safecrackers. Both these actors maintained a Caine-like work-rate during the Seventies, making about two or three movies a year. Some of these movies were standouts, but most were pretty ropey, and *Harry and Walter* falls into the latter category. And neither could match Caine's unflagging pace in the Eighties, when the careers of both actors tapered off drastically.

Diane Keaton appeared in the token-female-interest Katharine Ross role as a spunky proto-feminist reporter. Caine was cast as a swanky gentleman safecracker called Adam Worth, whom Harry and Walter beat to the loot in the climactic Big Bank Robbery. Director Mark Rydell (whose career peaked in 1981 with *On Golden Pond* – if you can call *On Golden Pond* a peak) announced, 'It's a Laurel and Hardy film with real people,' though compared to Caan and Gould here, Laurel and Hardy seem like masters of understated, sophisticated wit. This was one of those productions in which everyone had a fine old time slapping their thighs at the brilliant ad-libbing on set, but on screen it ends up as frantic mugging which is embarrassing to behold. Rydell encourages his performers to act *funny* and makes no attempt to curb their excesses. Even Caine, after a promising opening in which he establishes the supercrook as a smoothy-chops charmer – 'Do you know what it's like to break into a bank at two o'clock in the morning? Every pore in your body tingles with the possibility of failure' – ends up yelling his head off in protracted shouting matches with Keaton. 'It was one of those films that was so much fun to do,' Caine said, 'and with such clever people, that it should be a good movie.' It wasn't. And a failed comedy is one of the most depressing things in the world.

Heavy-handed hi-jinx in period costume; Caine with James Caan, Elliott Gould and Diane Keaton in **Harry and Walter Go To New York**

Throughout the first half of the Seventies there was intense speculation about whether or not Caine would become a tax exile, especially after Chancellor Denis Healey had made his famous 'we are going to soak the rich' speech. The rich felt that, with a top tax rate around the ninety per cent mark, they were already being soaked, and were practically queuing to leave the country. Richard Burton had already gone to Switzerland, Sean Connery to Spain, Peter Sellers to France, Rod Stewart and Mick Jagger to the United States. Roger Moore and Glenda Jackson stayed put. Caine declared repeatedly that he was also going to stand his ground, but eventually had to admit defeat and in 1977 he and his family packed up and set sail for Beverly Hills. 'I love my country and I want to live in it,' he said, 'but I have no intention of standing by and watching everything I've worked for taken away.' You can't really blame him. That year, the *Evening News* had reported his annual income as approximately £700,000 – reduced after tax to something in the region of £35,000. 'I'm perfectly happy to pay about fifty per cent,' he would say a few years later, 'for the care of the elderly and education and medicine and so on. But not ninety-two per cent. I do work hard, and I want my rewards.'

Another factor, far from negligible, was that after the short-lived boom years of the Sixties, Swinging London, Hammer horror and the New English Realism had all passed their sell-by dates. 'One of the reasons tourists came here in the 1960s was the image of Britain presented by the films and records of those days,' said Caine. But now the British Film Industry, deprived of most of its American backing, was in an even worse state of crisis than usual, and the number of film roles on offer in Britain was dwindling. 'The government has brought in new tax laws for people who go to England to make international pictures. The opportunities of these type of pictures have dried up.' Formidable though Caine's work-rate was, he worried he would be reduced to appearing in what he referred to as *I Was a Window-Cleaner's Underpants*. 'I never take my trousers off anyway,' he added.

For an English-speaking screen actor, Hollywood was where the work was.

20

THE CURSE OF SWITZERLAND

Silver Bears, adopted from Paul Erdman's novel of the same name, falls between two stools. On the one hand, it is a relic of the Sixties caper movie, of which Caine appeared in three very different variations: *Gambit, Deadfall* and *The Italian Job.* On the other hand, it anticipates the high-finance wheeler-dealers of the following decade who cropped up in films such as *Rollover* (Jane Fonda and Kris Kristofferson watching the collapse of the entire Western economy) and *Wall Street* (arrogant yuppie Charlie Sheen in thrall to Machiavellian financial wizard Michael Douglas).

Despite a story which embraces the Mafia, millions of dollars and a large smuggling operation, *Silver Bears* is resolutely lighthearted; no-one gets beaten up, let alone fitted for cement boots. The worst that happens is when a Californian banker (played by comedian Tom Smothers) takes the rap for everyone else's sins and winds up with a three-year prison sentence – but even then he is shown to be enjoying his incarceration.

Caine plays Doc Fletcher, a Mafia frontman assigned to supervise the purchase of a Swiss bank so his employers can launder money at their leisure. Louis Jourdan, as the impoverished Prince Gianfranco Pietro Annunzio di Siracusa, cons him into backing a silver mine run by David Warner and Stéphane Audran. (Audran, when she meets Caine, asks him, 'Dr Fletcher, what are you a doctor of?' To which he replies, 'Money.') After all manner of complicated financial shenanigans, the mine is exposed as a gigantic scam, though not before everyone has managed to make huge amounts of money out of it. Caine winds up owning the Swiss bank, and we are led to assume that he will henceforth go straight and settle down. Cybill Shepherd (career still reeling from a string of mid-Seventies flops, and yet to prove herself an acceptable light comedienne in *Moonlighting*) plays almost incidental love interest in what she obviously believes is a character role because she wears Harry Palmer spectacles for it. And there are drawbacks to character roles; Stéphane Audran gets to wear outré Karl Lagerfeld, but poor Cybill has to make do with gauche Californian ponchos and jangly charm bracelets.

Mafia boss Martin Balsam introduces Doc Fletcher with the line, 'He's not a fag, he's English,' and Caine goes on to deliver his standard Leading Man act – a caper hero who has neither past nor motivation but who simply exists. In the course of the film, he rides a donkey, has a wet shirt interlude in a swimming-pool, and a drunk scene when he thinks he is going to lose his beloved bank, and a pretty good snogging session on a bed with Cybill, who livens things up by wearing stripey socks. There is also an extended bout of driving slowly around a square in Lugano; the car is a convertible, and it is definitely Caine sitting in the driver's seat. So either the producers obtained special dispensation from the Swiss Ministry of Transport allowing the non-driving actor to take the wheel on a public highway, or there is a very small stunt-driver squashed out of sight under the dashboard.

Apart from brief excursions to Las Vegas, Carnaby Street and Morocco (standing in for Iran), the film was shot in Switzerland, and its overall tone is all-purpose Swiss bland. Switzerland's most memorable contribution to film culture was in *The Third Man,* when Harry Lime dismissed it as a nation of cuckoo-clocks. Ivan Passer, the Czech director who had co-written *Closely Observed Trains* and who went on to make the excellent *Cutter's Way* in 1981, manages with something approaching true genius to disguise the talkiness and lack of action, so at least the plot keeps moving and the picturesque scenery flits past painlessly.

The *Evening Standard,* mindful of *Silver Bears'* subject matter, reported that while on location, Caine had the latest share prices and exchange rates phoned to him from London every evening. 'I take an interest in everything political and economic,' he said, 'because I know it is going to affect me, and I like to stay ahead of the game.'

During the Seventies, newspapers couldn't resist sounding Caine out about his political leanings. He inclined towards the Liberal with a capital L, he said, and voiced antipathy towards paternal Socialism, Communism and East Germany. When someone asked him if he were a 'champagne Socialist', he replied, 'I suppose I am.' Later, in America, he described his politics as 'completely down the middle of the road, which is why I like the American Democrats.' By 1987, however, his allegiance had shifted, and he was wanting the Conservatives to win the General Election.

An uncomfortable ride for Caine and David Warner in **Silver Bears**

Only a year or so later, the Curse of Switzerland struck again. *Ashanti* (1979) takes place in Africa, but was financed by Swiss companies. Until you've actually had to sit through this piece of hogwash, it sounds irresistible; if not the *Citizen Kane* of its era, then at least something which falls into the category of an entertaining Bad Movie, like *The Swarm* or *The Holcroft Covenant*. In the event, it turns out to be the sort of film which cries out for adverbial abuse: staggeringly inept and brain-numbingly boring. Caine declared afterwards that it was the only film he had ever made purely for mercenary reasons; he had sold the Mill House (to Jimmy Page of Led Zeppelin, whose drummer John Bonham died there of an overdose not long afterwards) and was in the process of buying a house in Beverly Hills, one that had been built by Woolworth heiress Barbara Hutton (once married to Cary Grant) for her son's twenty-first birthday present.

In *Ashanti* he plays Dr David Linderby, whose dark-skinned wife Anansa (played by ex-model Beverly Johnson) does the sort of idiotic thing characters in slasher movies are always doing prior to being horribly murdered; she goes skinny-dipping in a strange lake. This is Africa, though, so instead of being hacked to pieces by a maniac with a knife, she is kidnapped by Peter Ustinov and his merry band of slave traders, who turn a deaf ear when she protests, 'I'm a medical doctor and I work for the United Nations.' Ustinov, oozing middle-eastern oiliness, talks with an accent midway between Nebuchadnezzar and Peter Sellers and says slimy things such as, 'There is inflation, even for virgins.'

There follows a transcontinental chase, with Caine becoming increasingly pink-faced and sweaty and gradually replacing the pieces of his pristine safari outfit with wrap-around native Arab gear. In his desperate quest, he is first joined by William Holden, who rapidly gets the hell out of the movie by crashing his helicopter into a river, and then by the mysterious, charismatic Arabian actor Kabir Bedi, who shows him the ways of the mysterious, charismatic Sahara desert. In other words, Caine has to learn that they cannot possibly adopt all the cute children they set free from all the slave traders they encounter and kill in their search for his missing wife. The cute children pluck at his wrap-around hem, clamouring to be taken home and loved. 'Stop it! Stop it!' shouts Caine, tears streaming down his face as, for once, he unwisely abandons his policy of underplaying big emotional moments. 'I can't take you with me! Don't you understand?' The children stare at this ranting, pink-faced foreigner, and look bemused.

Caine's other big scene is with a camel. Camels, like horses, gave him a hard time; he had already had bad experiences with camels on *The Man Who Would Be King,* when Sean Connery had cunningly swapped the beasts around so Caine ended up with the bad-tempered one. In *Ashanti,* there is the horrible feeling that it's not a stuntman who is filmed tumbling from the animal's back. Caine has a tough time trying to remount until Kabir Bedi teaches him to say 'Hut-ut-ut' when he wants the camel to be nice to him. But a high incidence of camel footage is not usually the indication of a successful movie, unless we're talking about Bob Hope and Bing Crosby in *The Road to Morocco* (some excellent talking camels in that one). More often, it is a reminder of such exercises in sand-locked dullness as *Ishtar* and *The Sheltering Sky.*

Much of *Ashanti* was shot in the Sinai Desert, which Caine decided, 'the Egyptians can have back as far as I'm concerned.' It was so hot that one of the camels fainted from the heat. Of all the films he'd made, he said, this was the hardest. It is also one of the hardest to watch. By the end, the viewer will be succumbing to desert fever and seeing tantalising mirages of *The Ipcress File* and *Get Carter* can-canning on the horizon, though the snazzy international soundtrack offers an intriguing foretaste of *Blame It On Rio.* For those who stick it out, there is a minor (a *very* minor) treat in store: Ustinov sells Anansa to none other than Caine's old friend from *The Last Valley,* Omar Sharif, in the role of a sleazy Panamanian prince who wants to make a present of her to his ailing father. 'Deplorable, but we must accept it,' he says upon learning that the woman is not a local virgin – as he has been led to believe – but a kidnapped married United Nations medical doctor from Boston, Massachusetts.

Suddenly, in its closing seconds, the picture stutters into something vaguely resembling life. Aboard his Panama-bound luxury yacht, Sharif insouciantly offers his captive a cucumber sandwich. Meanwhile, Caine and Kabir Bedi are zooming to the rescue in a speed-boat. Caine's mysterious, charismatic co-star sacrifices his life for the couple, who jump overboard and swim towards each other through a sea of starcrossed filters. And not before time.

'I did it solely for the money, and I have never been so unhappy in my career,' said Caine. 'I swore I would never do it again, no matter how broke I was.'

21

WEST COAST

California Suite (1978) was one of Caine's occasional appearances in the film of a hit play. This one was written by Neil Simon and already produced on Broadway; it breaks down into four separate storylines with nothing to connect them apart from their prime location – the Beverly Hills Hotel in Los Angeles.

The American East Coast-West Coast cultural divide is a favourite subject of Manhattanites such as Woody Allen, who makes all his films in New York and takes potshots at Los Angeles in *Annie Hall* and *Hannah and Her Sisters.* In *California Suite,* Simon, who had himself just moved from East Coast to West, plays off snappy New York-style wisecracking and heavyweight theatrical prestige against the tackiness of Hollywood, the vulgarity of the Los Angeles lifestyle and its social highlight, the Oscar ceremony. It is a measure of Michael Caine's versatility that he seems equally at home in either territory: movie-star glitz, and upmarket intellectual artiness.

Caine offers Maggie Smith a spoonful of caviar in their **California Suite**

Leading the East Coast contingent in one of the sections of *California Suite* is Jane Fonda as a chain-smoking, heavy-drinking, self-styled Dorothy Parker type who is visiting Beverly Hills to lure her daughter away from LA-based ex-husband Alan Alda – this seems rather perverse casting since Fonda is the epitome of non-smoking California Woman, and Alda looks and acts like the native New Yorker he is. Two of the film's other episodes are played purely for laughs, with the result that they're not very funny at all. One involves Bill Cosby and Richard Pryor as feuding doctors from Chicago. The other features Walter Matthau, in town for his nephew's bar mitzvah, as a married man who must find a way of removing the drunk blonde from his bed before his wife (actress and film-maker Elaine May, who directed the ill-starred *Ishtar*) turns up and sees her.

Caine plays Sidney Cochran, an antiques dealer visiting Los Angeles in the company of his wife – celebrated English stage actress Diana Barrie, played by celebrated English stage actress Maggie Smith – who has been nominated for an Oscar. They fling witty, bitchy, stagey dialogue at each other, the sort of dialogue around which actors love to wrap their laughing tackle. As Caine tells it, Neil Simon visited the set and said, 'Listen, if you think of anything funny, you know, ad libs, put 'em in. But tell me what they are first. And they better be funnier than what I've written.' Caine reports that he and Smith thought and thought, and never ad-libbed a word.

On the big night, the Oscar goes to another actress, Diana gets drunk and all the old skeletons come rattling out of the closet. Sidney prefers men to women and doesn't make love to his wife as often as she would like him to. Today such bisexuality would set alarm bells jangling in the heads of AIDS-conscious women, and this instantly marks down *California Suite* as a period piece, set in those long-gone, pre-*Fatal Attraction* days when infidelity wasn't a matter of life and death.

Eventually the couple's differences are reconciled, as we get the impression they have been reconciled on other occasions, and their genuine affection for each other is reaffirmed, though Sidney looks as if he would rather keep their relationship platonic.

It is really Maggie Smith's show, which leaves Caine providing unselfish back-up and giving good reaction in a white polo-neck. Smith even gets the Drunk Scene, something which usually goes to Caine, as well as plenty of nerves, neurosis ('If I'm not up by nine, I've overdosed') and snatches of great-actress theatricality. It seems a part tailor-written to impress the Hollywood yobs, and sure enough, in real life Smith landed the Academy Award that didn't go to her in the script.

The *Daily Mirror* heralded the film with the headline CAINE GOES GAY (BUT HE IS ONLY TAKING THE MICHAEL). 'It's the first time I've never researched a role thoroughly,' he told the *Daily Express*. But it turned out to be one of his favourite performances. 'I tried to get away from the whoops dear limp-wrist, and show a man in some pain,' he said. 'I got a letter from the chairperson of some Gay Association in the States, thanking me for portraying a gay without ridicule. I rather cherish that. Specially not being gay myself.'

Many leading actors would have been wary of playing a homosexual, but it was another indication that Caine, secure in his own self-image, was willing to take risks in his work. Not only was he confident of his straight reputation, he said, but he didn't care what people thought anyway.

If the British press was tolerant about his choice of roles, they were still taking a few digs at his decision to leave the country and live in Los Angeles – an action seen by some journalists as a betrayal of the British people. In the *Daily Express,* William Hickey reported that Caine was entertaining American television audiences by running down Britain on chat shows. The actor had apparently said that the British preferred *Land of Hope and Glory* to the National Anthem. 'Trouble is,' he went on, 'there is very little hope and not much glory.'

Exactly one month later, Margaret Thatcher became Prime Minister.

22

DISASTERS

One of the Seventies' most endearing contributions to world culture was the Disaster Movie. The recipe was simple: collect as many famous film-stars as you can afford, subject them to ordeal by special effects, and then, in reverse order of star magnitude, kill off all but the highest-paid players. The more celebrity deaths, the better. The special effects could be anything from a flood (*Flood!*), or an avalanche (*Avalanche*) to an earthquake (*Earthquake*), though in exceptional circumstances such as a meteor (*Meteor*), the special effects department might be required to conjure up a *compound disaster* and pelt the unfortunate characters with floods, avalanches, *and* earthquakes, all in the same film. As one can see, not a lot of imagination went into the choice of the titles, though the makers of the 1969 prototype disaster movie *Krakatoa, East of Java* (volcano, tidal wave) exercised a certain amount of artistic licence since Krakatoa is actually *west* of Java.

To bee or not to bee; Caine ponders the question with Henry Fonda in **The Swarm**

So one might say that the Disaster Movie was *Grand Hotel* with knobs on, though perhaps *Grand Hotel* with a collapsing ceiling and plummeting elevator would be nearer the mark. Most noteworthy of the bunch were probably *Airport* and its three sequels – *Grand*

Hotel in mid-air, plus jeopardy – and *The Towering Inferno* – *Grand Hotel* in a blazing skyscraper, boasting the starriest stars (fireman Steve McQueen and architect Paul Newman vying for top billing), and the most spectacular celebrity deaths (Robert Wagner goes up in flames, Richard Chamberlain takes a one-hundred-and-thirty-eight-storey dive). Film theorists have offered a variety of reasons for the popularity of disaster movies, some of them involving oil shortages and the collapse of the economy, but the most likely explanation for the fad was that same urge which makes people want to stare at the aftermath of a car crash, or read detailed newspaper reports of fatal accidents – a ghoulish fascination sometimes attributed to a 'There but for the grace of God go I . . .' reaction, or a desire to flirt with death without ever having to kiss it full on the lips. The Disaster Movie caters to those compulsions while minimising the guilt factor; viewers can take comfort in the knowledge that they are not gloating over the deaths of real people, though they don't seem to mind sitting in on the twilights of some very illustrious acting careers. Charlton Heston, Ava Gardner, Fred Astaire and Gloria Swanson all flirted with disaster at one time or another, though the unacknowledged champion of the form must be Henry Fonda, who appeared in no less than five assorted catastrophes. Hardline disaster aficionados, meanwhile, cherish a special fondness for Leslie Nielson, who later spoofed his own disaster-prone persona in *Airplane*.

The popularity of the Disaster Movie waned after its Seventies heyday, but even now it is far from extinct, though the form has mutated so it is not always instantly recognisable. *Die Hard* and *Die Hard 2*, for instance, are no more than our old friends *The Towering Inferno* and *Airport* disguised in modish trappings – megalomaniac villains, an arsenal of Kalashnikovs, and Bruce Willis in a vest, while recent films such as *Arachnophobia*, *Always* and *The Abyss* (and that's just the beginning of the alphabet) all have a touch of Disaster about them. But the Disaster Movie was already mutating back in 1978, when Michael Caine made his Disaster debut. *The Swarm* is a cross-breed of the classic disaster format with the Nature Bites Back subgenre initiated by *Jaws* (the one about the shark) and propagated by the likes of *Grizzly* (the one about the bear) and *Dogs* (the one about – yes! – the dogs). The film's distributors went to town on a multi-million dollar promotion which cost half as much again of the film's twelve million dollar budget. The director and producer was Irwin Allen, the 'Master of Disaster' who had also been responsible for *The Poseidon Adventure* and *The Towering Inferno*; in an interview before the premiere, he announced, 'I think *The*

Swarm is going to be the most terrifying movie ever made.' How wrong can a man be?

As one can *just about* gather from the title, *The Swarm* is about a swarm – of bees. These are African killer bees which – the film-makers assure their audience in a bid to forestall anti-bee hysteria and the indignant wrath of apiarists – bear no resemblance to 'the industrious American Honey bee'. These ferocious unAmerican hordes buzz-bomb Texas, stinging schoolchildren and picnickers to death before their *pièce de resistance* rockets the film's body count into the stratosphere – in an excess of bee cunning, they blow up a nuclear power plant. The city of Houston is then flambéed for dessert.

Caine plays the nominal hero of this saga: hunky he-man entomologist Brad Crane, who tracks the bees to a US Air Force Missile Base, where he is treated with suspicion by General Richard Widmark and his men. After a glittering roster of celebrity deaths (Ben Johnson, Fred MacMurray and Olivia de Havilland all die together when the bees cause a train crash; Henry Fonda snuffs it trying to find a cure for the killer bee-sting), Crane eventually sees the bees off by luring them into the Gulf of Mexico with the missile base's warning system (which just happens to sound like a bee mating call) and setting fire to the pesky little critters with flame-throwers. Not only does Caine provide the key to the bees' demise, he also gets the girl, in the shape of Katharine Ross. Richard Widmark gets most of the best lines, though; 'Houston on fire!' he exclaims at one point. 'Will history blame me . . . or the bees?'

The film was greeted with a universal thumbs-down, although most of the critics admitted they had found it a hoot. This was more than could be said for Caine's next venture into Disaster territory, another Irwin Allen masterpiece, called *Beyond the Poseidon Adventure.* The selling-point of the original *Poseidon Adventure,* released in 1972, was that the famous film-stars, led by ranting Gene Hackman, had to find their way out of an ocean liner turned upside-down by a freak wave; an irresistible notion to anyone who has ever gazed at the ceiling and wondered what walking across it would be like. Seven years later, *Beyond the Poseidon Adventure* virtually ignores this central gimmick; the characters might just as well be trapped in a building, or down a mineshaft, or in a ship that hasn't been turned upside-down. The big bee flop had obviously depleted Irwin Allen's resources because this time around Michael Caine is the starriest film-star on the Poseidon's passenger list; not even Henry *Disaster Is My Middle Name* Fonda is there to back him up. Instead of faded Hollywood greats, he gets support from interesting but

Caine goes **Beyond the Poseidon Adventure** *while Karl Malden and Telly Savalas look on.*

only moderately famous character actors such as Peter Boyle and Jack Warden.

Caine plays Captain Mike Turner, a salvage tug skipper who enters the ship through a hole in the hull with the intention of looting the safe. Jewels and money fall by the wayside, however, when he encounters an assortment of trapped passengers and proves he has a heart of gold by leading them all to safety. Sally Field goes along for the ramble and to provide a bit of extra-curricular chirpiness. Their exodus is hampered by illegal arms dealer Telly Savalas, making a return to the sort of villainous roles in which he specialised before *Kojak*. No-one seems to think it strange that the rest of the world appears to have abandoned the stricken liner, even though it appears to be swarming with trapped survivors.

Beyond the Poseidon Adventure didn't even have the saving grace of *The Swarm's* unintentional comedy, and several critics were beginning to question Caine's career choices. The actor explained his double flirtation with Disaster Movies by saying he had just moved to Hollywood and needed the work. Another of his justifications was that he had wanted to work in a big Hollywood special effects picture, and this might well have seemed a prudent move at this time – after *Star Wars* and *Close Encounters of the Third Kind,* special effects were becoming so prominent in mainstream movies that actors were having to learn to live with them. Besides, he interpreted it as a challenge; 'Trying to make something of the rather cardboard characters in those movies is quite difficult,' he said.

The Swarm and *Beyond the Poseidon Adventure* were not the first turkeys in which Caine had appeared – you would be hard pressed to find fans of *The Romantic Englishwoman,* for example – but it was the unapologetic, high-profile schlockiness of the two Disaster projects which was a major factor in winning him a reputation as an actor who was willing to appear in any old rubbish. Also, it was perceived to be the worst sort of rubbish: rubbish of the *American* kind, produced purely for commercial reasons and without the slightest pretensions towards artistic quality, though there are those of us who would prefer American rubbish over British rubbish any day, since most American culture springs from the unabashed trash ethic anyway – buy it, try it and chuck it away.

But Caine had arrived in Hollywood during an awkward transition period, both for the industry and for himself. While he was getting older, audiences were getting younger. Family films were a rarity, while the Seventies flush of intelligent adult drama (*The Godfather, Chinatown, All the President's Men*) was gradually giving way to films which would cash in on the popularity of *Saturday Night Fever, National Lampoon's Animal House* or *Halloween;* a slew of lame-brained teen musicals, vulgar frat-house comedies, and slice 'n' dice shockers, all aimed at teenage filmgoers. It was a vicious circle: demographic studies indicated audiences were getting younger; studios consequently aimed their films at younger audiences; *ergo,* fewer adults went to the cinema and audiences continued to consist of younger people. What was Caine, now in his mid-forties, to do? He was getting a bit old for straight action roles, though he would never have let his age or non-athletic physique stand in the way of charging about as though his life depended on it. And he wasn't in with the arty, intellectual American film-makers, although his performance in *California Suite* should have been a more than adequate calling card. At this stage, Woody Allen was still seven years away.

Caine did what he had to do. He worked.

23

SHOCK HORROR

Caine said, 'I heard that one of the reasons I got *The Island* was that an executive's wife had seen me in *The Swarm* and had told her husband, "This man has carried that picture all on his own. If he can carry *that,* then he can carry *this.*"'

After *Beyond the Poseidon Adventure,* Caine dived into another watery yarn. *The Island* – book and screenplay – was written by Peter Benchley, author of *Jaws* and *The Deep.* Although the leading role was offered to other actors (including Anthony Hopkins) Benchley said he had always had Caine in mind for it. Blair Maynard is a crusading journalist who turns Action Man when the going gets tough. Estranged from his wife, he is forced to take his young son Justin along on a voyage to investigate the mysterious disappearances in the Bermuda Triangle. Justin, who has been whingeing about not being taken to Disneyworld, soon finds himself plunged into a real-life adventure which leaves Peter Pan at the starting-post.

After encounters with some wacky characters (a gung-ho gun salesman, an eccentric doctor, a pilot who blithely lands his plane with the undercarriage up), father and son are kidnapped by genuine, cutlass-wielding, eyeball-rolling, oogh-arrghing pirates. David Warner, their captain, hails Justin as the descendant of the man who killed Blackbeard, adopts him as his own, and rechristens him Tue-Barbe. Caine, meanwhile, is put to work impregnating the island's only healthy female – Australian actress Angela Punch McGregor in deconstructed Laura Ashley and matching mudpack. Even her get-up pales into insignificance, though, when compared to the fishnet tights and hair-curlers of that fine British actor Dudley Sutton, as the nuttiest of the buccaneers.

Rarely has there been such a rum load of old pirates as this lot. They mutter and burble, sounding as if they're constantly tanked up on home brew. Their behaviour exhibits all the symptoms of several centuries of inbreeding, and they seem to be having trouble with their syntax; 'What also else what you saw?' asks one of them, while another contributes the memorable line, 'He drownded for certain.' And for certain what also you know Justin will never be truly integrated into the buccaneering way of life so long as he says things like, 'May I lead the hunt?'

The eccentric doctor turns out to be the pirates' benefactor. 'An anthropologist's dream,' he prattles to a handcuffed Caine. 'You're witnessing the 17th Century.' Caine doesn't seem too thrilled at being plonked in the middle of this natural paradise full of uncorrupted real men. After several abortive attempts to escape (including one break for freedom which is curtailed by a wrestling match with a giant squid) he finally manages to reach a coast guard vessel, where he mows down the entire rollicking crew with a sustained burst of machine-gunfire. All, that is, except Warner, who urges Justin to shoot his father. The boy, however, is beginning to have second thoughts about spending the rest of his life with a bunch of Long John Silver impersonators. Either that, or he decides to back the winning side, which is Caine, who kills Warner with a flare gun. The Coast Guards are left to mop up the mess. 'There appear to be some coast guard casualties,' says a helicopter pilot as he hovers over the corpse-strewn boat. 'The rest are . . . the best I can describe is some sort of *civilian*.'

One might say *The Island* was ahead of its time. Only a few years later, the screen would be bursting with failed pirate movies: *The Pirate Movie, The Pirates of Penzance, Yellowbeard* and *Pirates*. Caine was at one point approached to play the central role in this last project, to be directed by Roman Polanski, but was reluctant to take it because it would have meant five months filming in Tunisia.

But perhaps one pirate movie is enough for any career. Caine's role involves a lot of heavy physical activity. He starts off in Harry Palmer spectacles, but is soon casting them aside to RUN through the vegetation, BLOW UP the buccaneers' ammo store and SWIM through squid-infested waters. There is a lot of swimming; Caine's hair takes on that permanently damp and curly look, and even when he's not ploughing through the surf, he's covered with a layer of anxious sweat. The use of Richard Strauss's *Heldenleben* on the soundtrack (augmenting a typically fine Ennio Morricone score) suggests that some meaningful subtexts were intended, but, in the end, the message boils down to an incisive criticism of the sort of foster parents who run around cutting throats, setting fire to schooners and cackling, '*Haar haaar!*'

The film was greeted by a chorus of derision from the critics, who were now becoming seriously worried about the direction Caine's career was taking at the start of the Eighties. Caine didn't appear to share their concern. 'I don't mind,' he said a few years later. 'I'm very well paid and I'm not worried. I seem to have the capacity for

Dudley Sutton (far left) and assorted buccaneers confront a captive Caine on **The Island**

survival, which although I didn't know it when I came into this business, is now the most important quality.'

Nevertheless, *The Island* is a lot of bloodthirsty fun, not all of it unintentional, and was directed with some gusto by Michael Ritchie, whose films are generally considered to have gone downhill since the mid-Seventies, when he made *Smile,* a satire of the American Way of Life set during a Californian beauty pageant. Yes, *The Island* is very, very silly, but then who said adventure stories were supposed to be credible, sensible, artistically sensitive meditations on the meaning of life?

Caine's next director was one of the American Movie Brats who had invaded Hollywood in the Seventies – film-makers who had grown up obsessed with cinema, and who now packed their own work with references and knowing nods towards the films they admired. Brian De Palma's first big hit was *Carrie* (1976), adapted from Stephen King's novel, in which emotionally unstable teenager Sissy Spacek uses her telekinetic powers to kill her bullying class-mates. De Palma followed this up with more telekinetic pyrotechnics in *The Fury,* which concluded with a memorable scene of villain John Cassavetes being blown to smithereens in slow-motion. De Palma's work had always borrowed freely from the films of Alfred Hitchcock, and his next big film, *Dressed To Kill* (1980), tipped its hat at *Psycho* with not one but two shower scenes, as well as a mad killer who turns out to be a transvestite.

If the Sixties were Caine's 'Harry Years', then the Eighties could be considered his 'Elliott Era'; Dr Robert Elliott in *Dressed to Kill* was the first of three characters he played within a few years of each other called Elliott (the runner-up is Sidney, with two name-checks). Dr Elliott is a psychoanalyst, one of whose patients – sexually frustrated housewife Angie Dickinson – is slashed to death in an elevator by a mysterious blonde in dark glasses. The doc is getting strange messages on his answering machine from 'Bobbi', apparently another of his patients, who wants a sex-change operation because he/she claims to be a woman trapped inside a man's body, 'and you're not helping me to get out'. 'Bobbi' also hints that she killed Dickinson with the doctor's own razor.

The dead woman's son (Keith Gordon) teams up with a witness to the murder (the director's then wife, Nancy Allen), a prostitute whose own life is now being threatened by the killer. Eventually – more by accident than design – they expose Dr Elliott as a transvestite transsexual (not from Transylvania, unfortunately) with a split personality. Dickinson had driven 'Bobbi' into a murderous fury by making a pass at Elliott and arousing the masculine side of his sexuality.

Though transvestite killers were nothing new after Anthony Perkins in *Psycho* and Rod Steiger in *No Way To Treat A Lady,* the ending of *Dressed To Kill* still came as a shock, thanks to Caine. He underplays his role as a psychoanalyst so successfully that it is only after he has been unmasked that one can appreciate his skill. On the second viewing and closer examination, the doctor appears to be such a hive of pent-up neuroses and repressed twitches, constantly staring at his own reflection, that it is difficult to imagine how one could have overlooked it the first time around. But the combination of De Palma's dazzling technique, Caine's leading man status, and some outrageous red herrings (a police woman who happens to dress *exactly* like the murderer, for instance) was enough to distract most audiences away from the obvious conclusion: that Dr Elliott had to be the killer, simply because there were no other likely suspects in the film.

When De Palma originally approached Caine to play the role, the actor thought, 'Why not? It's a risk, but it could work.' Though it was his stand-in, a very tall stunt girl wearing a false nose, who actually wielded the razor in the murder scene, the actor himself had to dress in women's clothing for the unmasking at the end, and was reassured to find he didn't enjoy it. He also had to assume an American accent for his voice recordings as 'Bobbi'. Caine thought De Palma a bit chilly as a person, but admired him as a director.

Dressed To Kill is full of flashy effects, and for one shot, incorporating nine pages of complicated medical dialogue and a three hundred and sixty degree swing of the camera on a staircase, Caine ended up doing twenty-six takes – a record for the actor who usually has it down in one. *Dressed To Kill* might be a triumph of technique over emotional content – but what technique!

Critics and audiences were suitably impressed and the film did good box-office; it was Caine's biggest success since he had crossed the Atlantic. Its release in Britain generated some controversy since the Yorkshire Ripper was still at large and movies such as this were thought to encourage violence towards women. It also led to a debate on morality, in that Dickinson's character is cut down just after committing adultery – a fate similar to many of the teenage victims of American slasher movies, who didn't seem able to have sex without being carved up by a maniac immediately afterwards. One would be hard-pressed to describe De Palma as a feminist, but if that had indeed been his view, he would surely not have cast so sympathetic an actress as Angie Dickinson in the role of the victim, nor would he have given her time and opportunity to give substance to her character.

Oliver Stone directed his first film, a bizarre Canadian horror fantasy called *Seizure*, in 1974. Seven years later, he was back on the horror trail with *The Hand*. Stone had already written the screenplay for *Midnight Express*, but it would be some years before he eventually hit the big time with the sort of politically-engaged movie (such as *Platoon*, *Wall Street* and *Born on the Fourth of July*) with the wham-bam style and clobbered-home liberal ethics which were to earn him such sobriquets as Oliver *Sublety Not My Middle Name* Stone. He is a man's man, not exactly known for his sensitive attitude to female characters, and *The Hand* is a primer of all the ideas about manhood and masculinity which inform his later work.

This was Michael Caine's first appearance in a straight horror movie, though *Dressed To Kill* had its gory moments. He plays Jonathan Lansdale, the successful creator of a Conanesque comic strip called Mandro (Stone also co-scripted the movie *Conan the Barbarian*). He lives in an idyllic lakeside retreat in Vermont with his wife and young daughter.

One day he loses his right hand in a freak car accident. Andrea Marcovicci, as the wife, is driving, while Caine is sitting in the passenger seat. They are engrossed in an argument about whether to move from their house into a New York loft for the winter. For some reason best known to himself, Caine has stuck his arm out of the window to signal to the following car, while somehow failing to notice there is an enormous great lorry just in front of them. *Whoops.* Stone goes to some considerable trouble to set up this incident, though at least he doesn't make the same gaffe as British author Marc Brandel (author of *The Lizard's Tail,* the book on which the screenplay was based), who had the character contrive to lose his *right* hand while driving a car with *left*-hand drive.

Strangely enough, no-one can find the severed extremity at the scene of the accident, so Lansdale has to make do with a stump and a strap-on prosthetic. There is more than just a hint that the loss is tantamount to loss of manhood and impotence. Naturally, his cartoon-drawing days are over, and with them, his ability to support his family. Meanwhile, his marriage is getting rockier by the minute, and is hardly improved by his reluctance to let his wife touch his stump. He tries teaching a drawing class out in California, but is haunted by black-and-white hallucinations in which his missing hand scuttles around behaving badly. One day it behaves *very badly indeed* and throttles a flirtatious female student, as well as a rather unlikely redneck psychologist.

Next, Mrs Lansdale announces she is having an affair with her yoga teacher, a man who addresses her as 'my dearest, darling spirit', and that she has converted Margaret to a macrobiotic diet. Her husband is understandably appalled by this cosmic twaddle. It comes as no surprise when she too is attacked by the rogue hand, which Caine chases out of the house and into the garage.

The scene that follows is the unrivalled highlight of the film. First the hand attaches itself to the back of Caine's neck and he staggers around yelling. Then he does some bar-room arm-wrestling (or perhaps that should be wrist-wrestling) with it, after which he tries to pry it loose with his teeth. Next, it scuttles up his trouserleg and delivers a deft blow to his private parts before clamping itself around his throat while he writhes on the floor attempting to dislodge it. Eventually he manages to stick a bread-knife into it and it hobbles off. This is marvellous stuff, all the better for being played dead straight. One wonders whether it was seen by budding film director Sam Raimi, who seven years later would insert a similar scene into *Evil Dead II,* but this time definitely played for laughs – the severed hand even smashes crockery over its former owner's head.

As far as the rest of the movie goes, it's virtually a one-man show, and Caine, as always, rises to the occasion. So does his hair, which starts off longish and vaguely bohemian, as befits an artist, but which gets wilder and woollier with every scene. As his obsession with the missing hand grows, so he becomes more unshaven and dishevelled. There is not a lot of ranting, but a fair amount of manic staring and melancholic brooding, and Stone keeps the whole thing on a suitably gloomy keel. Eventually, the corpses of the hand's two victims are discovered mouldering in the boot of the cartoonist's car and it becomes apparent, as if we hadn't already guessed, that the hand is *all in his mind;* he has been blacking out and committing the murders himself. In an epilogue, we see him with electrodes taped to his forehead in what is presumably a mental hospital while a doctor, played by Viveca Lindfors, explains that the hand is *all in his mind.* In a daft, last-minute twist, the hand pops up and murders her while its erstwhile owner looks on, laughing hysterically.

The Hand's most famous precursor was, of course, the 1946 film *The Beast with Five Fingers,* in which Peter Lorre has a similar running battle with a severed extremity. There is a slight problem, from a film-maker's point of view, in that it is difficult to take a scuttling hand seriously as a viable movie monster. What can a single hand do, after all, apart from lurk and launch itself at people's throats? Waggle its finger dauntingly? Play the one-handed piano concerto Ravel wrote for Wittgenstein's one-armed brother? (In the Lorre film, the hand plays Bach.) The American critics didn't care for the film, and it barely saw the light of day in Britain, where it eventually limped out on a video release. But Caine's refusal to play his role for easy sympathy makes it an effective depiction of one man's mental disintegration as a result of his being able to get to grips (literally) with his feelings. In his later, more commercially successful films, Stone might have gone on to wrestle with the problems of being a macho man in a macho man's world, but he never ventured quite so near the knuckle as he did here. Sometimes by accident, horror films have a habit of reaching the parts that other films dare not touch.

24

FOOTBALL

Caine's next role taxed the credulity of even his most indulgent fans. Michael Caine? A West Ham United and England International *footballer?* Even at the beginning of his career one could never have described his physique as athletic. After his early years of hardship, he had not exactly stinted on the good life, and now he was nearly fifty. His performance in *Escape to Victory* presents a credibility gap in a way that active roles such as those in *Beyond the Poseidon Adventure* or *The Island* do not; Captain Mike Turner and Blair Maynard were not supposed to be professional sportsmen. Luckily for him, the film being set in 1943, his football kit was not as peek-a-boo as the form-hugging shorts worn by players nowadays.

Caine plays prisoner-of-war Captain John Colby in this World War II yarn which makes *Roy of the Rovers* look like hard-hitting realism by comparison. The director was Caine's old pal John Huston, who was never above interleaving his very best films (*The Man Who Would Be King, Wise Blood, The Dead* . . .) with some mind-boggling bummers (*Phobia, Annie* . . .). In its wacked-out way, however, *Escape to Victory* is of passing curiosity value, not least for its gaggle of ageing soccer stars (Pelé, Bobby Moore, Mike Summerbee) who are wheeled on to give some *bona fide* kick to the action. Pelé 'choreographed' the moves in the big game. Osvaldo Ardiles also puts in an appearance, and sharp-eyed football addicts with long memories might also be able to spot members of the 1980 Ipswich Town squad.

The plot hinges on German High Command's dubious scheme to win a propaganda war by having a team of German internationals knock the stuffing out of an Allied POW eleven, in front of a crowd of occupied French – dubious because anyone with half a brain could think of a more foolproof, rather less complicated method of peddling a pro-German message to the masses. The Allied team, naturally enough, seizes the opportunity to escape, though not before – and here one's jaw is apt to drop a couple of miles – *refusing to make a break for it until they have made up a 4-1 deficit.* The luckless French resistance has spent half the movie tunnelling through the sewers to get to the Allied dressing-rooms, but all to no avail – the Allies opt for the more salubrious method of disappearing into the crowd at the end of the match.

Max Von Sydow plays the token honourable German who recognises Caine as a famous England international. 'It's a shame the war has ended your career,' he says. 'If nations could settle their differences on the football pitch, wouldn't that be a challenge?' Of course, from an English point of view, this is precisely what the English and West German teams have been doing ever since the 1966 World Cup Final, and *Escape to Victory* merely confirms English prejudices by having the German players fling themselves to the ground and roll around in fake agony as soon as they come within sniffing distance of the penalty area.

There is a token American too, and he happens to be played by Sylvester Stallone, who between takes kept dashing back to his trailer to write the screenplay for *Rocky III.* Caine and Stallone, by all accounts, got along famously during the making of the film, which was shot in Budapest – the only European city to possess a suitable stadium without floodlights. Both actors had struggled to escape from tough, working-class backgrounds, but, as *Escape To Victory* emphasises, their approaches to acting are completely different. While Caine applies himself to his role with his usual no-fuss diligence, Stallone's part has been beefed up to allow him to demonstrate heroism appropriate to one of his megastar status. Firstly, he undertakes not one but two risky escapes. Secondly, he has to have his customary being-kicked-in-the-head scene. Thirdly, he has to exchange yearning glances with a female member of the French resistance, as if to prove that incarceration in a prisoner-of-war camp hasn't had too damaging an effect on his hormones. Lastly, and most important, he must win the match for the Allies. There were a few problems with this last proviso since he was playing the goalkeeper. Stallone apparently wanted to storm up the pitch and boot the winning goal into the back of the net, but a compromise was eventually reached and he saves a penalty instead.

Whereas American movie-makers have frequently celebrated their national games on film (especially baseball, which cropped up in *Field of Dreams, Bull Durham, Major League, Eight Men Out* and *The Natural*), British sports have never had too much coverage on celluloid, and there is no real British equivalent of the way in which respected American writers (Norman Mailer, Bernard Malamud, Joyce Carol Oates and so on) have embraced sport as part of their intellectual culture and national heritage. The British national game has never been celebrated on the big screen. Whatever its

Caine plotting tactics in
Escape to Victory

shortcomings (and there are bucketsful) *Escape to Victory* is a rarity; a film about football, though one assumes that most fans would probably find a live league game more dramatically exciting than a fictionalised film which delivers the action in heavily edited snippets.

A career in football is one of the acknowledged ways for working-class boys to surmount their humble origins; Caine took a different route. Perhaps surprisingly, for one born and bred in East London, he supports neither West Ham United nor Millwall. He has in the past declared his allegiance to Chelsea.

Deathtrap, starring Michael Caine and directed by Sidney Lumet, is not to be confused with *Death Trap,* directed by Tobe *Texas Chainsaw Massacre* Hooper, in which crazed Louisiana hotel-owner Neville Brand feeds guests to his pet crocodile, though police sometimes failed to make the distinction when they raided video shops during the mid-Eighties furore over the so-called 'Video Nasties'. Many discerning film fans, however, would plump for Hooper's film over Lumet's any day. Lumet is one of those directors much loved by serious-minded cinephiles but whose reputation tends to rest more on heavyweight past work (*Twelve Angry Men, Dog Day Afternoon*) than on duff recent outings such as *Family Business*.

Lumet's *Deathtrap* is a return to the unabashed theatricality of *Sleuth*. It is adapted from the hit play by Ira Levin, author of *Rosemary's Baby* and *The Boys From Brazil* and well-known for his careful attention to plotting. Sure enough *Deathtrap* turns out to be all plot and not a whole lot else. It calls for a slightly bigger cast than *Sleuth*, but at core it's another two-hander taking place in a single set. Dyan Cannon lasts up to the end of Act One before being killed off, and Irene Worth pops up every so often as a nosy psychic neighbour, but mostly the drama rests on the shoulders of Caine and his co-star Christopher *Superman* Reeve. In a shock-horror twist which must have left middlebrow audiences gasping in the stalls, these two are revealed to be homosexual lovers. In the scene for which the film is still best remembered, the actors clamp their mouths together for a man-to-man kiss which got the tabloid press all hot under the collar. The *Sun* duly responded with a suitably poetic burst of alliteration: MY CISSY SCREEN SMACKER, BY CAINE.

This time, Caine is in what one might term the Olivier Role: that of a scheming playwright called Sidney Bruhl, with Reeve as the upstart whippersnapper who is muscling in on his territory. Caine remarked approvingly that Bruhl was 'mad, stark raving mad. It's a lovely role,' and wastes no time at all in getting to his now obligatory Drunk Scene; at the beginning of the film, after his fourth successive flop, Bruhl is drowning his sorrows, convinced he has lost the golden touch which made him the toast of Broadway. He tells his neurotic wife (Cannon) that he has invited one of his former students (Reeve) to their swanky Hamptons home (characters in this sort of play *always* live in swanky homes) with the intention of murdering him and stealing the play he has written.

Reeve is apparently murdered, but returns from the grave and frightens Mrs Bruhl – who just happens to have a weak heart – to death. But of course it is all a scheme so that her husband will inherit her money – and yes, the weak-hearted wives *always* have pots of money in this sort of play. Then comes the 'cissy screen smacker', which Caine and Reeve did in one take, afterwards assuring curious journalists that they had had to drink a whole bottle of brandy before summoning courage for the scene and, no, they hadn't enjoyed it, honestly they hadn't. Caine later joked that he'd told Reeve, 'If you open your mouth I'll kill you.'

The story winds down into a battle of wits between the two lovers. Reeve, pretending to be Caine's 'secretary', moves into the house and starts writing a play called *Deathtrap.* Caine, sensing blackmail in the air, plots to murder him, Reeve turns the tables, and so on. The crosses and double-crosses pile up until, ultimately, one wishes they would hurry up and cross each other out.

Deathtrap is the sort of film which tends to be considered prestigious by people who don't like films all that much. Like *Sleuth,* it's aimed at audiences who adore Agatha Christie-type mysteries in which the convoluted plot takes precedence. It revels in clever-clever dialogue, relies heavily on absurd contrivance, and gives its performers a chance to let their hair down and ham it up in the best traditions of the proscenium arch.

Lumet filmed in long takes, and the result is even more theatrical than *Sleuth.* But whatever the film's faults, it was another of those roles which enhanced Caine's reputation, allowing him to show off his skill with words, and the critics were suitably impressed, considering it a great improvement on his other recent roles. It also underlined his willingness to take risks; most Hollywood actors would be wary of playing a homosexual man once, however juicy the role, and this was the second time he had done it. And with several solidly filmed plays under his belt, Caine has managed to give the impression of taking the theatre in his stride without actually having had to tread the boards since the early Sixties. Just occasionally, he would be tempted to go back to the stage; he was offered the Broadway lead of *Romantic Comedy* by Bernard Slade, but turned it down because there was no guarantee of his being able to play the lead in the film version (it eventually went to Dudley Moore, and the film turned out to be one of his floppier flops).

25

THREE GREAT PERFORMANCES

When asked about his acting technique, Caine will say he concentrates hard and works out everything well in advance. 'But I don't take it home with me,' he says. 'I can switch on and off. You have to if you're a film actor, otherwise your home life would be hell.'

If Caine were a Method Actor, his home life would be particularly hellish since he doesn't mind playing characters who are unpleasant or unsympathetic, not to mention psychotic. But for his role as Dr Frank Bryant in *Educating Rita,* he went in for some atypical physical preparation by deliberately gaining thirty-seven pounds in weight. And he did it with no fuss, with none of the publicity which attended Robert De Niro's fattening up for *Raging Bull.* He did it so well and so quietly that his old friend Terence Stamp expressed concern about his health, saying he looked off-colour. Caine took this as a sign that the performance had worked. 'To tell you the truth, I'm worried about Tel,' he responded in an interview with Chris Peachment of *Time Out,* 'I tell you, the boy's got so thin lately he can hardly lift a bag of brown rice.'

The role of Dr Frank Bryant was one of his all-time favourites, and won him his third Oscar nomination. 1983 was the year all but one of the Best Actor nominees were British (the others were Tom Conti for *Reuben, Reuben,* and Albert Finney and Tom Courtenay for *The Dresser*) but the award went to the token American, Robert Duvall, for his performance as a country and western singer in *Tender Mercies.* Duvall was great in the role, but the award might also have been something of a backlash against the British contingent, which had taken Best Film two years running with *Chariots of Fire* and *Gandhi.* For *Educating Rita,* Caine had to make do with sharing a BAFTA award with Dustin Hoffman's drag act in *Tootsie.*

But though Caine's performance is a joy to watch, the film itself is nothing to write home about. It's the screen adaptation of a theatrical two-hander, Willy Russell's play about a working-class hairdresser called Rita who wants to break free from the restrictions of her background by taking an Open University course, in English Literature. Lewis Gilbert directs efficiently, and at least manages to lose the appearance of theatricality which (perhaps intentionally) made *Sleuth* and *Deathtrap* so stage-ridden.

But *Educating Rita's* theatrical origins are betrayed by the nature of its dialogue; these are not real people speaking, but mouthpieces, characters who have been created expressly to put across two sides of an argument, and the minor characters, who seem to have been tacked on in an effort to 'open out' the play, are never more than one-dimensional caricatures. As with *Alfie,* Caine's other collaboration with Gilbert, we might as well be listening to a radio play. One can't fault the two stars, however. Caine, in particular, manages to invest his character with a life which extends beyond the limits of the screen. This is a Great Movie Performance, even if it isn't a Great Movie.

Columbia Pictures, the film's backers, wanted Dolly Parton for the role of Rita, but Gilbert held out for Julie Walters, who had played the role on stage. The film was shot in and around the quadrangles of Trinity College, Dublin, partly because tax regulations prevented Caine from spending more than ninety days a year in England.

Frank Bryant is a college tutor, a cynical, failed poet with a crumbling marriage and a fondness for the bottle. He teaches his pupil that Eng Lit is as much a matter of learning how to pass exams as anything else. In return, she encourages him to pick himself up out of the wreckage of his life. It is all very schematic, and somewhere in the middle the tutor starts behaving like Professor Higgins, bemoaning the way his creation appears to be getting on fine without him. Caine, however, considered the story to be less *Pygmalion* and more *The Blue Angel,* with Bryant fascinated by the earthy, life-affirming, non-intellectual vulgarity of his pupil.

Afterwards, Caine said he based the character partly on playwright Robert Bolt, and partly on Peter Langan, Caine's business partner in Langan's Brasserie, a restaurant they had founded together in the early Seventies. 'I'm a big noisy man who needs lots of space,' Caine said. 'So I picked another big noisy man, Langan, and we made it our own. I love it. I would eat there all the time even if I didn't own the place.' Langan's wasn't his only venture into the restaurant business, and in 1978, he put money into The London Club, a little corner of England on La Cienega Boulevard in Los Angeles, where British expatriates could gorge themselves on hotpot, steak and kidney pie, and bangers and mash.

Before it was made, *Educating Rita* was regarded in some quarters as 'the girl's picture', but Caine recognised it as a perfect opportunity for him to demonstrate one of the things at which he shines –

reaction, which comes across on screen much better than it does on stage – and he is unfailingly generous in support of Walters. He also found the escaping-from-one's-disadvantaged-background story close to his heart. 'In real life, I was Rita,' he told a reporter. 'When you're working-class, everybody expects you to be stupid. If you're halfway bright, which I was, everyone falls about with surprise.'

Unfortunately, Willy Russell goes out of his way at the beginning of the film to make Rita appear very stupid indeed. For instance, when her tutor asks her if she is familiar with Yeats, all she can say is 'The wine lodge?' – and she isn't joking. The middle-classes listen to classical music and live in houses with plain walls and tasteful Habitat-style furniture; they are cultured but prone to adultery and suicide attempts. The working-classes get their kicks from communal sing-songs in the local pub, the interior walls of their homes are covered with non-U wallpaper, and they despise learning so thoroughly that they are not above a spot of book-burning if their wives get too chummy with the likes of Chekhov.

For dedicated Caine-watchers, *Educating Rita* forms a diptych with *The Honorary Consul:* though the characters are very different, both roles virtually consist of one long Drunk Scene. Caine has always remembered the advice of a director who once told him that drunks don't walk crookedly and talk in slurry voices, but speak and move very deliberately, constantly fighting to stay in control. And no-one is quite like Michael Caine when it comes to conveying all the varying *degrees* of drunkenness. There's Dr Bryant's normal, everyday tippling from a bottle of whisky stowed behind a copy of (what else?) *The Lost Weekend.* Then there are his attempts to keep upright while way over the limit ('Of course I'm drunk – you don't really expect me to teach this when I'm sober?'). And then there is that most extreme stage where, upset that Rita no longer seems to need him, he has got himself completely legless, so stewed he can barely tell the difference between disco-dancing and keeling over. Shambling, out of shape, Caine is magnificent, conveying an entire history of dashed hopes and self-indulgent wallowing behind his scraggy beard and booze-reddened complexion.

The Honorary Consul pitted Caine against Richard Gere, an actor whose golden boy good looks ensure that he is consistently being underrated by critics. Shortly before shooting, he was propelled by the success of *An Officer and a Gentleman* into super-sex-symbol status, and it would be nearly a decade before he would live it down, proving his versatility with a swift double: light romantic

Julie Walters gives Caine a haircut in **Educating Rita**

lead in *Pretty Woman,* heavyweight villain in *Internal Affairs.* It has to be admitted, however, that he is miscast as Dr Eduardo Plarr, the half-British, half-Paraguayan protagonist of Graham Greene's novel. Gere's hair-do is too Californian, his appearance too much a feature of his acting style, and his acting style too laid-back to suggest the inner turmoil of a typical Greene hero. And there is a touch too much posing against Venetian blinds, as if the director (John Mackenzie) had seen *American Gigolo* too many times and been impressed for all the wrong reasons.

No such complaints about Caine, however, who was undertaking his second great boozy role of 1983: Charley Fortnum, the Honorary Consul of the title. Unfortunately, it was felt by the film's distributors, 20th Century Fox, that American audiences wouldn't know their consul from their elbow, so for the US release the title was changed to *Beyond the Limit,* which perhaps deserves some sort of prize as one of the least catchy, least memorable, least descriptive titles of the decade.

Caine is first glimpsed slumped on the floor of a bar and blaming his drunkenness on the unusually large Latin American measures. Later, after the plot of the film has been laid out at a snail's pace, he is kidnapped by a hamfisted bunch of revolutionaries who think they have bagged themselves the visiting American ambassador as a hostage. Fortnum, on the other hand, is 'pitiably small beer', and nobody will lift a finger to get him back. Gere, who is having an affair with Caine's young wife, finds himself dragged into the situation against his will, and, after realising he is jealous of the consul's capacity to feel love, even unrequited love, dies a useless death at the hands of the police. Caine is restored to his wife, who is expecting the dead doctor's child.

It is a symptom of the plodding ineptitude of Christopher Hampton's screenplay that Greene's original book *starts off* at a point which doesn't come until halfway through the film. I am not suggesting for a second that film adaptations are improved by remaining faithful to their source material – in many cases, the opposite holds true – but here it seems almost perverse to replace the book's narrative economy with a sprawling, literal re-enactment of relationships which Greene managed to establish with a few sentences.

Never mind: it's another Caine performance to savour, another of his Englishmen Abroad, and he adds a desperately-needed touch of humour to the film, looking as if butter wouldn't melt as he swaps his hipflask for a bottle of Coca-Cola, or tra-la-laing selections from *Carmen* as he weaves down the road in his jeep. His

Charley Fortnum is a pathetic shell of a man who gradually recovers his dignity under pressure and who finally comes to some sort of an understanding with himself and his wife.

This is also the first time Caine acted with Bob Hoskins, who plays Colonel Perez, the Chief of Police. Hoskins starred in another John Mackenzie film, *The Long Good Friday,* as a character not a million miles away from Jack Carter. Hoskins, like Caine, built an acting career out of a broad London accent, and has succeeded in landing some plum roles in the United States (*The Cotton Club, Who Framed Roger Rabbit?*).

After putting on all that weight for *Educating Rita,* Caine suddenly found he had to lose it – and fast. For *Blame It On Rio* he would be required to strip off and roll in the sand with a sexy teenager less than half his age. Caine enjoyed the Brazilian locations, especially immediately after filming *The Honorary Consul* in Mexico. He had no complaints about Mexican efficiency, he said, 'but there is a problem with a lot of sickness from the food, which is the wonderful thing about Brazil – you don't get sick.'

Bring up the subject of *Blame It On Rio* in serious film-buff company and you will be greeted by a barrage of groans. The director was the legendary Stanley Donen, responsible for some of the best-loved musicals of the Fifties (*Singin' in the Rain* for one) as well as some of the wittiest, most stylish entertainments of the Sixties (the comedy-thriller *Charade,* for example). But the Seventies and Eighties were not fruitful decades for Donen, and *Blame It On Rio,* his last film, looks like the movie of an old man trying to be a swinger.

The plot was lifted wholesale from the 1977 French comedy *Un Moment d'Égarement (One Wild Moment)* directed by Claude Berri of *Jean de Florette* fame. Hollywood is forever plundering the French cinema for hit films to remake in the American style, which usually means all moral and social ambiguity to be ironed out and replaced with an extra-big dollop of squishy American sentiment. Thus, *Un Éléphant ça Trompe Énormément* became *The Woman in Red, Cousin, Cousine* was reduced to *Cousins,* and *Trois Hommes et un Couffin* wound up as *Three Men and a Baby.* Now when it comes to frothy comedies about sex, the French have a head-start; they know how to do these things properly there – perhaps it has something to do with the cuisine, or maybe adultery is simply the natural by-product of a bourgeois society. But what may seem irresistibly sophisticated when accompanied by subtitles is apt to come across as irredeemably tacky and tasteless when rehashed in the American idiom.

Caine plays Matthew Hollis, a middle-aged businessman who embarks on a holiday in Rio de Janeiro with his friend and business partner Victor. Both men are having problems with their marriages, Matthew's wife having announced at the last minute that she will be taking *her* holiday elsewhere, and on her own. Matthew's daughter Nicole and Victor's daughter Jennifer accompany their fathers; both girls are nubile teenagers who whip off their bikini tops and scamper through the surf the minute they hit the beach.

After some exquisite travelogue footage of hang-gliding and carnival revelling, Matthew finds the wine, the whirling colours, and those wild Brazilian bongo rhythms all going to his head. Before he knows what's hit him, Jennifer has zoned in on him and they are making mad passionate love on the sand. Now he has to conceal their affair from the angry and possessive Victor, who knows something is going on without realising that his friend is the man involved. Cue for a lot of French farcing around, recriminations, fisticuffs, and the unexpected arrival of Matthew's wife, who confesses she and Victor have also been having an affair. Eventually, husbands and wives get back together, and the girls end up sticking to chaps their own age.

Blame It On Rio might have been an interesting attempt to deal with that rather creepy middle-aged male fascination with teenage girls whose bodies are more mature than their minds, had it not been for one disastrous bit of casting, which instantly tips the film over into being just another example of that middle-aged male fascination *in action*. Caine, excellent as usual, is ably backed up by Joseph Bologna and the intriguing Demi Moore, prickly and vulnerable as Nicole. There are one or two hints that Matthew's fling with Jennifer is the expression of an unrealised desire to get to know his daughter better, even incestuously, but this line is rapidly shut down as a notion too dodgy for decent folks to contemplate (decent folks evidently have no trouble with middle-aged men having affairs with *daughter substitutes*) and the character of Nicole gets rudely shunted aside as not important to the plot.

In the role of Jennifer, however, ex-model Michelle Johnson is no more than a mindless, curvaceous wet dream; a big-bosomed cutie who throws herself at Matthew with the take-me-I-worship-you attitude of the total male fantasy. Write this stuff up and you could probably get it published in *Men Only*. Admittedly, Johnson hasn't received an awful lot of help from her scriptwriters, who fail to grant her the slightest scruples about worrying her father, upsetting her friend, delivering the *coup de grace* to her lover's troubled marriage, generally disrupting other people's lives and ruining their holiday, and finally attempting suicide because she is not getting her own way. Unfortunately the suicide attempt is botched, but the depth of Jennifer's feelings for Matthew can be gauged by the manner in which she promptly falls for the first young Latin American stud she set eyes on.

Caine, though, gives it all he's got. 'I did it in order to prove that I could do comedy,' he said, 'and with the reviews I got for it, I proved I could do comedy.' Eighteen years after *Alfie,* in 'confessional' inserts of the characters reminiscing about their experiences as though describing them to an amiable marriage guidance counsellor, he once again demonstrates the art of speaking straight to camera as though he really meant it. And this is one actor who doesn't look as if he even bothers to work out, but that doesn't mean he's embarrassed into keeping his body under wraps; gamely he peels his clothes off whenever the screenplay demands it, even stripping down to his underpants for an extended cathartic buddy-buddy tussle with Bologna after everyone's dirty secrets have tumbled out into the open – about as near as Caine has ever got to the nude wrestling scene which dissuaded him from taking a role in *Women In Love.*

While he is well-preserved for a man of fifty-one, it isn't a particularly pretty sight by film-star standards: still slightly flabby around the midriff even after a concerted pineapple-and-water diet, not very muscular, a bit pasty. And yet, by most other standards, it is a most agreeable sight. Michael Caine in underpants is about as real as you can get – he could be anyone's husband or father, he could be *you.* This is not a body that has been synthetically pumped-up in a Beverly Hills gymnasium. Supreme self-confidence is not necessarily the mighty-biceped Mr Universe look of Arnold Schwarzenegger or Sylvester Stallone – it's a man who is so comfortable with himself he doesn't need to build a superbody to stand between him and the rest of the world. Caine is about as honest as an actor can get, and still *be* an actor. Whether squirting toothpaste on his pyjamas or looking embarrassed in the midst of a bevy of half-naked dancing girls, he is a class act, and one the film doesn't really deserve.

Susan George and Caine (in cunning vicar disguise) duck for cover in **The Jigsaw Man**

26

THREE DOGS

In the mid-Seventies, Caine was cast in the role of Kim Philby, though Philby himself was reported to have been miffed at the idea of being impersonated by someone he sniffily referred to as a 'jumped-up milkman'. Caine eventually had to back out and was replaced by Robert Shaw, and Don Sharp took over from Mike Hodges as director, but it was not to be, and it wasn't until the early Eighties that Caine was cast in *The Jigsaw Man* as 'Sir Philip Kimberley', a former Director-General of the British Secret Service who has defected to Moscow.

The film begins in surreal fashion, with Michael Caine's voice coming out of a mouth belonging to someone who is most definitely *not* Michael Caine – not even Michael Caine in an ingenious Milo Tindle-style disguise with lots of peel-off pieces of rubber. As we stare in bewilderment, this man is accused of getting drunk at state banquets and kissing a Soviet minister 'on the lips'. Aha, this sounds more like the Caine we know and love, a retread of *Deathtrap* perhaps, but the next thing we know, the man with Michael Caine's voice is being carted off into the operating theatre for a dramatic *Seconds*-style rejuvenation.

Eventually the bandages come off, and Michael Caine (for it is he) looks at himself in the mirror and says, 'Christ.' As well he might; Russian plastic surgery has changed him from a sixty-two-year-old into a forty-two-year-old played by a fifty-year-old. Caine immediately grows a moustache and gets down to a serious training montage, in which he develops his karate, cycling and punchbag skills. Egged on by a man called Boris who tells him to pedal faster, he visibly mouths the words 'fuck off'. One wonders whether this was in the original script.

Unfortunately, the rest of the film fails to live up to this rip-roaring opening. Kimberley, now posing as Soviet superspy Sergei Kuzminsky, is sent back to England to recover a missing dossier. The minute he lands at Heathrow he shakes off his Soviet minders by defecting and adopting a fake Russian accent (ie, instead of saying 'your people', he says 'your pipple'). Next, he shakes off his English minders (including his old buddy Laurence Olivier, who understandably fails to recognise him), gets shot, and drips blood all the way to meet his daughter – the very wonderful Susan George, still wearing Sixties-style pale lipstick. George's big screen debut had been in *Billion Dollar Brain,* as a Russian girl who sits next to Harry Palmer on a train and offers him an egg.

'You can't go around like this,' says Sir Philip's daughter, dressing his wound in a pastoral lakeside setting.

'I'll go to a chemist, in town,' he says.

The film is full of rapier-sharp exchanges like this. In a later scene, he asks his daughter, 'What do women use to change the colour of their hair?'

'Shampoo rinse,' she replies.

'Shampoo rinse?' he asks.

'Yes,' she says, 'you can buy it at the chemist.'

By now, the viewer is panting in anticipation of the Great Chemist Scene, but it never happens. What we do get, however, is the KGB rolling up the wrong girl in a carpet and whisking her off to Moscow as a hostage; this ill-starred character is never seen or heard of again. The film gets sillier and sillier, but unfortunately not silly enough to be thoroughly entertaining, though Caine does his best, speaking with an Oklahoma accent to stop a gullible bobby giving him a parking ticket, disguising himself as a vicar, and karate-chopping an innocent man to death *by mistake.* There is also an inordinate amount of driving around; confirmed Caine-watchers will have fun trying to ascertain whether this film was shot before or after the actor finally took and passed his driving test.

The plot thickens. Robert Powell, who hitherto has been posing as a member of the 'narcotics division' of the United Nations, turns out to be working for MI6. Charles Gray, who has been posing as a member of MI6, turns out to be working for the KGB. The script, which has been posing as a low-key Le Carré-type intrigue, turns out to be a light-hearted *New Avengers* chase thriller. Or is it? It's not easy to tell, and it can't have helped that the money ran out before the end of the filming, Olivier took his lawyers' advice and walked off the set because he hadn't been paid, and the last six days' shooting was postponed until six months later. (It is symptomatic of Caine's career that he managed to turn out two leading performances in the interim.) Poor old Terence Young, who had directed the first two Bond films, was saddled with the impossible task of trying to fit the pieces of *The Jigsaw Man* together. The film went straight to video.

Water gave Caine a role which was more or less the comic version of Charley Fortnum from *The Honorary Consul,* but the film is so botched it somehow manages to make the Graham Greene adaptation seem a laff-riot by comparison. Caine plays Baxter Thwaites, governor of the Caribbean island of Cascara, a small British dependency which has been totally forgotten by Whitehall until the resident singing freedom fighter, played by Billy Connolly, attempts to enlist the help of Cuba in his struggle for independence. Leonard Rossiter is promptly dispatched from Whitehall to forestall trouble by closing the dependency down and evacuating its population. Matters are complicated by the last-minute discovery that the island is a source of valuable mineral water. American drilling companies, environmental activists, saboteurs hired by a rival mineral water company in France, and media all converge on the tiny blob of land. Exploiting the publicity, Billy Connolly stages a Concert for Cascara at the United Nations, and the island duly gains its independence. The saboteurs succeed in destroying the mineral water supply, but the islanders subsequently strike oil.

Water was scripted by Dick Clement and Ian La Frenais, who made a name for themselves writing television sitcoms (but who had also scripted films such as *Villain,* a rough, tough gangster movie with Richard Burton). Bill Persky had a hand in the script, but Clement also directed and La Frenais produced, so it really is all their fault. Their best TV work has been based on believable characters, rooted in real-life situations, and interpreted by superb comic actors: James Bolam and Rodney Bewes as the beer-guzzling Bob and Terry in *The Likely Lads,* or Ronnie Barker as the cunning old lag Fletch in *Porridge.* The duo's recent big screen ventures; however, have been disastrous. Working for cinema, it is as though

An Englishman abroad; Caine as the governor of a Caribbean island in **Water**

they suddenly forget what makes their small screen work so successful. *Water* (like *Bullshot* and *Vice Versa*), replaces all those recognisable situations with out-and-out whimsy, and ditches all that careful character study in favour of mile-wide caricature. Leonard Rossiter, for example, is encouraged to saunter through another one of his Whitehall bureaucrat acts, while Brenda Vaccaro, as Caine's party-mad wife Dolores, performs at a pitch of constant semi-hysteria which is tiring to behold.

There are echoes in the story of *Whisky Galore* and *Passport to Pimlico*, but the execution is flabby and soft-centred, like an Ealing comedy with its teeth extracted – and Ealing comedies were not exactly known for their savage bite in the first place. Events reach their absolute nadir in the Concert for Cascara, when Billy Connolly is joined on stage by ageing rockers Ringo Starr, Eric Clapton and George Harrison (executive producer of Handmade Films, which backed this fiasco). It's the same old story; about the only thing the film has going for it is Michael Caine.

As the peace-loving governor, whose idea of fun is to sit around smoking dope, Caine stands as the still centre of a whirlwind, and emerges once again with his reputation intact. The more his co-stars roll their eyeballs and yell in a desperate attempt to be funny,

Caine holds up the screenplay of **The Holcroft Covenant***; someone has already thrown a rotten tomato at it*

the more he underplays and steals the show. Halfway through the film, he is suddenly required to swap his flowered shirts for khaki fatigues and bullet belt and take to the hills as a freedom-fighting guerrilla – the screenplay has done nothing to prepare us for this, but Caine takes it in his stride. If *Water* never quite tips all the way over into being utterly unwatchable, it is all due to him.

Three days after washing his hands of *Water,* Caine accepted an offer to star in *The Holcroft Covenant* when James Caan dropped out because of health reasons and disagreements with the producers. The screenplay was adapted from a Robert Ludlum novel, one of those chunky tomes with daft, meaningless titles which clog up the book-shelves at international airports. (The same author's *The Osterman Weekend* was filmed by Sam Peckinpah in 1983.) The director, John Frankenheimer, had in the past honed the political paranoia thriller to a sharp point in *The Manchurian Candidate,* adapted from Richard Condon's novel. And George Axelrod, who had written that script, came into the *Holcroft* production to add polish.

Frankenheimer said Michael Caine was the best actor he'd ever worked with. Caine plays Noel Holcroft, architect and 'foreign-born American citizen' who is summoned to Geneva and told he has inherited four and a half billion dollars of ex-Nazi loot from his father, a Nazi officer who committed suicide at the end of the war. Holcroft must get together with the eldest sons of the two other dead Nazis to sign the appropriate documents and make sure that the money will be used for the good of mankind and not for nefarious neo-Nazi purposes.

No sooner has Holcroft been informed of all this, then people start dropping like flies all around him; two in Geneva, another in his apartment building in New York. He begins to get suspicious. He flies to London (no wonder these books are always on sale in airports) and meets Victoria Tennant, daughter of one of the dead Nazis. She introduces him to her brother, Anthony Andrews, who writes 'brilliant but mysterious articles on international finance for the *Guardian*'. Unbeknownst to Holcroft, he is also the leader of a worldwide neo-Nazi conspiracy and is having an affair with his sister. Just in case we don't think that's evil enough, he kills a dog, a man in a wheelchair, *and* – only minutes after praising her potato salad – Holcroft's mother.

Holcroft, meanwhile, has flown to Berlin with Victoria and been kicked in the groin by a transvestite. He recovers sufficiently to make amorous advances to Victoria, however, to which she responds with the words, 'No . . . no . . . *yes!*' This is just one of the film's hilarious low-points. Even better is the way in which the characters choose the most bizarre and exposed locations possible in which to deliver enormous great chunks of vital plot-exposition to one other and the audience: the middle of Trafalgar Square, an all-night horse-riding school, and slap-bang in front of the Brandenburg Gate, after which someone asks, 'Should we be standing out here in the open like this?'

The third and last dead Nazi's son turns out to be a world-famous conductor. Anthony Andrews then reawakens the Curse of Switzerland by advising everyone to 'drive to Geneva' and 'take the back roads as much as possible'. The covenant is signed, but Holcroft has alerted the media and spills the beans. In not one, but *two* separate struggles with revolvers, the world-famous conductor and the financial correspondent of the *Guardian* are both shot dead. Holcroft, who has deduced that Victoria is not be trusted, courteously allows her to blow her own brains out.

The screening of *The Holcroft Covenant* was one of the strangest film previews I have ever attended. The beginning of the film was greeted with a respectful hush considered appropriate for the work of a director of Frankenheimer's standing. As the story unfolded there was a slight fidgeting as the audience realised they were being served up with a load of old codswallop. Finally, as the plot skewed off in ever more ridiculous directions and the dialogue became more and more risible, the preview audience gave up all pretence at reasoned, critical sobriety and rolled around in the aisles slapping their thighs, shrieking with laughter and shouting unruly comments at the screen.

Of all the stinkers in which Caine has appeared, *The Holcroft Covenant* rivals *The Swarm* as one of the most hilarious, and should be ardently sought out by anyone who treasures a truly bad movie. Caine spends most of the film saying, 'I don't believe this, I do not believe what I am hearing,' and 'There are people who are actually trying to kill us.' There are meaningless and protracted discussions about umbrellas, a series of spectacularly inept assassination attempts (one would-be hitman knocks over five pedestrians and wrecks a shopfront, while somehow managing to miss his target), and a brilliant scene in which Caine explains why he can't drive a car; there's no point when you live in New York, the traffic's terrible, you can't park etc. Victoria snaps at him, 'Do you realise you're endangering our lives by your incompetence?'

Ironically, the actor had finally passed his driving test. 'I learned in three lessons,' he said. 'My instructor said he knew I'd learn very quickly because I was an actor. He said, "The minute you got in the car you took on the role of an expert driver – and of course you were."' Caine had certainly spent a fair chunk of his career sitting in drivers' seats, trying to look as if he knew what he was doing. In Los Angeles, he bought a Rolls-Royce which was variously described as 'beige' and 'champagne-coloured'. 'What people forget is that out here the temperature in a black Rolls is considerably higher than in a light-coloured one,' he said.

Caine goes respectable and wins an Oscar for Best Supporting Actor; with Mia Farrow in **Hannah and Her Sisters**

27

AMERICAN INDEPENDENTS

Hannah and Her Sisters (1986) is Woody Allen (no relation to Irwin Allen) in schizophrenic mode. 'My goal with *Hannah* was to combine a deep poignancy with hilarious comedy in a great family saga,' he said, being serious yet not being serious. Like *Manhattan,* his most perfectly realised movie, *Hannah and Her Sisters* combines the art house angst of his po-faced homages to Ingmar Bergman with the humour of films such as *Annie Hall,* in which cultural name-dropping rubs noses with intellectual slapstick. Unlike *Manhattan,* it doesn't achieve the perfect balance, although there is no question it was his most entertaining film in years. Allen has always had trouble assimilating these two sides of himself – he apparently labours under the notion that comedy can never be 'serious'. Hence his films tend to divide easily into crowd-pleasing diversions full of jokey neuroses and cultural name-dropping, and angst-ridden gloom-fests in which the characters dress in colour co-ordinated knitwear and go around behaving as if they're going to slit their wrists at any minute.

Hannah and Her Sisters is in fact only partly about Hannah and her sisters, played by Mia Farrow, Barbara Hershey and Dianne Wiest; it is also about the men in their lives, and here, Allen divides his alter-ego into three separate characters. Firstly, he himself plays his familiar loveable schlemiel, Hannah's ex-husband, a hypochondriac TV writer who becomes convinced he has a brain tumour. Secondly, there is the ghost of the Gloomy Swede himself, Ingmar Bergman, in the shape of Bergman's favourite actor, Max Von Sydow; he is an artist living with Hannah's sister Lee (Hershey), and the sort of cheerful chap who will greet her with the line, 'You missed a very dull programme about Auschwitz.' Lastly, there is Michael Caine as Hannah's husband Elliott, an investment banker who is apparently happily married, but who is so besotted with his sister-in-law Lee that he is prepared to risk a coronary by running several Manhattan blocks in order to bump into her 'accidentally'.

'It was just like working with a family,' Caine said of filming *Hannah and Her Sisters*. Mia Farrow, whose mother was played by her real-life mother Maureen O'Sullivan, had been Woody Allen's partner and muse for most of the Eighties, and large chunks of the film were shot in her apartment. André Previn, Farrow's ex-husband, also turned up on set just in time for a scene in which Michael and Mia were in bed together, which Caine said he found rather embarrassing.

It might vaguely occur to the viewer to wonder what a down-to-earth Londoner like Caine is doing in the company of all these middle-class New Yorkers who like to witter endlessly on about their relationships and whose financial problems are limited to deciding whether or not to lend large sums of money to one another – this is fairytale never-never Manhattan, all winter sunlight, gallery openings and string quartets, and never a crazed crack-addict nor a sociopathic mugger in sight. (Hannah's household is run by a black maid, though of course it is Hannah herself who gets all the praise for being such a super hostess.) Caine is so good, however, that the audience is soon accepting him as a natural extension of the Woody Allen stock acting company. And *voilà* – there he is, wrapped in a chunky oatmeal cardigan like the best of them, comparing Barbara Hershey to a poem by e.e. cummings, and bending the ear of his psychoanalyst as though he'd been doing it all his life.

And only Caine could get away with playing such an unsympathetic character and yet still remain likeable. Elliott, as the romantic klutz nervously in pursuit of the object of his obsession, acts as a vessel for all the negative traits which Allen is wary of taking on board in the characters he himself plays, doling them out instead so his alter-egos take the rap for him while he remains love-able. 'God, I'm despicable,' says Elliott in another of his voice-overs – 'What a cruel and shallow thing to do.' Elliott gives in to his adulterous urges with barely a struggle, determinedly plots his pursuit of Lee without pausing to consider the effect his attentions are likely to have on her, allows himself to suffer a modicum of hypocritical guilt by way of expiation and finally ends up smug and self-satisfied, his relationship with Hannah stronger than ever despite his boorish behaviour. But, though these may be weaknesses, they are also signs of humanity, and no-one is better than Caine at bringing out the human side of a character, reminding us that in real life, unlike fiction, people are not divided exclusively into good and bad but are complicated mixtures of both.

'Woody choosing me to do *Hannah* made me respectable as a comic actor,' Caine said afterwards. He was made even more 're-spectable' after the Oscar ceremony. After having been nominated as Best Actor for *Alfie, Sleuth* and *Educating Rita,* he finally won the Best Supporting Actor award for *Hannah,* beating Tom Berenger and Willem Dafoe (for *Platoon*), Dennis Hopper (for *Hoosiers* aka *Best Shot*) and Denholm Elliott (for *A Room with a View*). It is not as though his performance in the Allen film was *better* than usual. It was just that *Hannah and Her Sisters* got him a lot more notice, was perceived as a prestigious slice of cinematic art, and as a suitably upmarket showcase for a fine actor to demonstrate his talent. He thoroughly deserved his Oscar, but perhaps it is not so difficult to give a terrific performance when your writer/director is a popular, critically-acclaimed film-maker. The mark of a major screen-actor is whether he can appear in utter dross and still emerge smelling of roses, with his reputation intact. 'I learn probably more from a bad script than I do from a good one,' Caine said.

Talking of dross, he was not present at the Oscar ceremony to collect his award for *Hannah and Her Sisters,* being contractually obliged to languish in the Bahamas for the filming of *Jaws – the Revenge.*

If Caine was getting pickier about his screenplays, it had less to do with quality than with location. 'When I open a script and it says, "Nome, Alaska. Our hero is walking in the blinding snow with a dog sled . . ." I close it again. Quickly.'

Writer/director/actor Alan Alda, one of Caine's co-stars from *California Suite* (though they didn't have any scenes together), phoned him and said, 'I've got just the part for you – a big-headed movie-star!' Alda added that shooting would be taking place all summer in the Hamptons, the swanky Long Island resort for rich Americans where *Deathtrap* playwright Sidney Bruhl was supposed to have lived, and that Caine would be able to stay in a house on the beach. The actor didn't hesitate.

Sweet Liberty tells the story of a film within a film. Alda cast himself as Michael Burgess, a naive academic whose weighty historical novel on the American War of Independence is being made into a movie by a big studio. When the film crew descends on its small-town location in North Carolina, he is horrified to discover that most of his serious research is being ditched by the director, who is replacing it with the three elements essential for the all-important appeal to the youth market: authority must be defied, property must be destroyed, and clothes must be taken off. Burgess hooks up with the screenwriter (Bob Hoskins with an American drawl) in a covert attempt to inject some tone and historical accuracy into the script, and tries to feed the results to the leading actors. Michelle Pfeiffer, as the actress playing Burgess's patriotic heroine, encourages his attentions, which she realises will help her role research, and he, confusing her with the character she is playing, falls in love.

The leading man is British actor Elliott James, a dashing lady-killer and confirmed daredevil with a passion for fast cars, helicopters and roller-coasters. Burgess, tailing around after him, suffers acute anxiety and physical discomfort before allowing the actor to thrash him at fencing. *Fencing* – the 31-year-old Michael Caine, giving his first interviews for an inquisitive press, had once lamented his lack of such essential actorly accomplishments as skiing, riding and fencing. All things come to those who wait – although Caine never did feel happy on the back of a horse; a riding scene in *The Holcroft Covenant* had to be amended, for his benefit, to a climbing-off-and-leading-the-horse-by-the-reins scene. To date, he has not been filmed on skis.

Sweet Liberty is amiable, undemanding entertainment, though Alda the director is sometimes guilty of precisely the sort of vulgarity for which he is satirising his fictional counterpart. Ninety-year-old Lillian Gish, in her one hundred and fourth film, is wheeled on as Burgess's bedridden mother to serve no discernible purpose before being wheeled off again, but Caine strolls through his role with the air of a man who has been handed an excellent gift and who is determined to make the most of it, even when forced to lead some of his co-stars in a rousing rendition of *Knees Up, Mother Brown*.

Caine as the evil Mortwell in **Mona Lisa**; *with Cathy Tyson*

28

BACK TO BRITAIN

Caine remembers some advice given to him by Peter O'Toole. Don't play small parts, even in big films, because that'll make you a small part actor. Play leading parts anywhere – in rubbish – but play leading parts.

And play leading roles he had done (apart from in his two big battle movies, *Battle of Britain* and *A Bridge Too Far*) until the mid-Eighties, when he took a small role in *Mona Lisa,* partly as a favour to his old pal Bob Hoskins. The role might have been small, however, but the character was not; it is the sort of part which requires someone of Caine's reputation to pull it off. He was on the set for only a week, but his menacing shadow dominates the film.

Hoskins is the heart of the film, a small-time crook called George who after a seven-year prison sentence comes home to South London to find himself cold-shouldered by his wife, though he manages on the sly to meet up with his school-age daughter. Associates of his former boss, Mortwell, fix him up with work delivering porno videos and chauffeuring Simone, a chic black prostitute, to and from the houses and hotels where she meets up with her wealthy clients. George falls in love with her, and agrees to help her find her friend Cathy, a young heroin addict. He finds her being abused by one of Mortwell's clients, and whisks her away; he and the girls flee to Brighton, where he realises Simone and Cathy are lovers and that Simone has just been using him all along. Mortwell arrives on the scene, and is promptly shot dead by Simone, who nearly shoots George as well. He returns to South London a sadder and wiser ex-con.

Mona Lisa is not exactly a *Get Carter* for the Eighties, but it might have been a punchy little gut-grabber if only its co-writers, David Leland and Neil Jordan, who also directed, had had enough confidence in his thriller material to let it speak for itself. Unfortunately, it is watered down with scenes between George and his eccentric friend Thomas, played by Robbie Coltrane, who provides an ironic running commentary on George's exploits, as if to distance both the film-maker and the audience from the plot. The result is a serious dissipation of the tension and dark mood which have been carefully built up elsewhere. There is also a debilitating whiff of subtext in the air. As in far too many British films, audiences are being told what the story is *about* instead of being left to work it out for themselves.

Caine, though, delivers one of his scariest performances as Mortwell. George gives him a white rabbit, and later we see him with the rabbit on his lap; the set-up is reminiscent of Ernst Stavro Blofield and his fluffy white cat – we are talking supervillains here. We don't actually *see* Mortwell doing anything evil until the end, when he hits Simone, but there is no question he is an evil man, capable of anything we could imagine, and probably worse. He lurks in the backrooms of corridors behind tacky bars and strip joints, questionable establishments one assumes he owns, simply because he *looks* as if he owns them. Or he holds sway in the Turkish bath, telling bad jokes to a crowd of hangers-on; around his neck there is a fat gold chain, like the necklace of a corrupt mayor, shouting Money and Power. When we first see him, he appears to be an affable fellow (too affable – he says the name *George* far too many times, as if by reciting it like a mantra he increases his power over the name's owner). But when he smiles, the smile doesn't reach his eyes – they stay cold and hard. Mortwell is one of those people you wouldn't care to bump into on a dark night.

Caine brushes up his culinary skills and gives Sigourney Weaver the Harry Palmer treatment in **Half Moon Street**

Half Moon Street might once have sounded promising. American Bob Swaim, fresh from the critical success of the tough French *policier, La Balance,* co-wrote and directed. The story, adapted from Paul Theroux's novel *Dr Slaughter,* starred Sigourney Weaver as Dr Lauren Slaughter, a Harvard PhD veteran of three years' fieldwork in China, arriving in London to start work at an institute for international affairs. The pay, however, is not good, and she is frustrated by the covert sexism which enables less-talented male colleagues to grab the plum assignments. In order to amass some extra cash and exchange her low-rent Notting Hill bedsit for something plusher, she decides to get a second job. Now, you or I would end up as a cashier in a twenty-four hour supermarket, or stuffing pieces of paper into envelopes, but not Dr Slaughter; she decides to moonlight as a high-class escort agency girl. Mostly this seems to involve dressing up in slinky outfits and dazzling her clients with brilliant and sophisticated repartee, but occasionally, we are given to understand, she slips between the sheets with them.

One of the people with whom she does her sheet-slipping is Lord Bulbeck, a lonely widower and Middle East troubleshooter played by none other than . . . Michael Caine. We know the two of them are intellectually well-matched because when they bump into each other at the greyhound track, she responds to his 'Let us go then, you and I,' with an impassioned, 'When the evening is spread out against the sky,' thus demonstrating they have read the same bit of

TS Eliot. All is not roses, however, because Lauren later finds out they share the same star sign and are therefore astrologically incompatible.

For one who is supposed to be so brainy, our heroine persists in behaving like a half-wit. Lord Bulbeck is enmeshed in incredibly heavy and hush-hush peace negotiations which will determine the fate of most of the Middle East – and yet she attributes his lack of full-time emotional commitment to social embarrassment. And she apparently expects him to drop everything, including his bodyguard, and nip over to Geneva with her for a dirty weekend. When Caine is unable to join her there, Weaver sleeps with a stranger in revenge. At the mention of Geneva, if not before, the viewer's heart will sink like a stone. Yes, the Curse of Switzerland strikes again.

Nor does she turn a hair when a Palestinian diplomat arranges for her to move into the luxurious Mayfair flat he is vacating, supposedly out of the goodness of his heart. It transpires, of course, that the Palestinian and his cohorts (including the stranger with whom she slept in Geneva – it's a small world) are plotting to murder both her and Bulbeck in order to destroy Bulbeck's reputation (presumably something like TOFF FOUND DEAD WITH DOXY IN LOVE NEST SHOCK HORROR). In what comes as rather an anti-climax, the security forces arrive in the nick of time, and though Dr Slaughter gets shot, the wound is unfortunately not mortal. Both she and Lord Bulbeck, one assumes, will live to recite TS Eliot at each other until the cows come home. The incredibly important Middle East peace negotiations, meanwhile, are apparently not so important after all, since the film comes to a full-stop before they can even take place.

In the book, Lord Bulbeck was in his seventies, and not so central to the plot. In the film, of course, his part has been expanded to fit Caine's star status, and the story ends up a rather conventional romance with an annoying heroine who thinks she is so bright when she is actually very stupid, and one or two stray social-political strands waving like unattached fronds in the background. The dialogue is embarrassing, never more so than when Dr Slaughter, finding the shower broken in her bedsit, shouts to her friendly black neighbour, 'Call the plumber, Lindsay or you'll have another Notting Hill riot on your hands – a *white* one!'

John Preston, hero of *The Fourth Protocol,* is not so very different from Harry Palmer, if you can imagine Palmer twenty years after *The Ipcress File,* a failed marriage and some middle-aged bulk under his belt, but still hacking his way through the restrictive red tape of

Spycatcher Caine in
The Fourth Protocol

British Intelligence and getting his bosses all worked up over his unorthodox *modus operandi.* Of course, he can't be bothered to cook for himself any more, and he really has no time at all for women.

Frederick Forsyth adapted his own novel for the screen, with the help of George Axlerod, who had evidently not been forced into early retirement by the universal chorus of jeers which had greeted *The Holcroft Covenant.* Caine joined Forsyth and Wafic Said as executive producer; John Mackenzie, who had directed *The Honorary Consul,* came in as director, and a heavyweight cast was assembled.

Pierce Brosnan is a fine actor who is probably not taken as seriously as he should be because of his classic good looks. There is enough cruelty hovering about his mouth to make one regret the contractual obligations to *Remington Steele* which prevented him from having a shot at James Bond. In *The Fourth Protocol* he plays KGB man Major Petrofsky, assigned by a rogue general to pose as an Englishman and foul up the Fourth Protocol (a treaty limiting the use of nuclear weapons) by detonating an atomic bomb at an American air base in East Anglia. The estate agent never once stops to ask why this mysterious and handsome non-American stranger should be so eager to rent a house with a bedroom looking out on to a load of noisy F1-11 strike bombers.

Caine's John Preston, of course, is the only man who can stop him, with or without the backing of secret service bigwigs such as Ian Richardson, Julian Glover and Michael Gough. Ned Beatty and Ray McAnally, in the obligatory fur hats, are their Soviet counterparts, and the KGB Colonel Joanna Cassidy provides Petrofsky with sexual relief besides tampering with his time-delay mechanism in order to set things up for a last-minute scrabble in the vicinity of the button.

Despite good performances from the all-star cast, *The Fourth Protocol* succumbs to terminal blandness, the characters are no more than pawns in service of the plot, and the plot itself shifts on to automatic pilot long before the mildly exciting climax. There are, however, a fair number of pleasures to be dug out and savoured by the tenacious film-goer. One can admire the wardrobe which Caine chose himself and which consists of standard spy equipment: poloneck, trenchcoat, padded anorak and leather jacket (not to be worn all at once). We also get the once-in-a-lifetime opportunity to watch Joanna Cassidy construct an atomic bomb out of a transistor radio,

Caine puts his best chin forward in **The Fourth Protocol**

some shoes and a pair of motorcycle headlamps (children – don't try this at home). And we wonder, for the umpteenth time, why Russians ever choose to become spies in the first place, since the casualty rate is alarmingly high; they are forever being ordered to kill one another off.

In his very first scene, Caine appears to be drunk, but it turns out he is only faking in order to break into someone's flat; with the Fake Drunk Scene, Caine adds a further refinement to his staggering repertoire of Degrees of Drunkenness (probably his most sustained Fake Drunk act can be seen in *The Whistle Blower*). After blowing a safe and exposing Anton Rodgers as a double-agent, he is confronted by outraged boss Julian Glover trotting out such tried and trusted outraged-boss-clichés as 'I'm well aware you somehow consider yourself as outside the normal chain of command . . .' and 'Look, Preston, let's get this straight . . .'

It soon becomes apparent that Caine's boss is either not very bright, or batting for the opposite side, or – more likely – both things at once. When Caine announces, 'That metal disc can only be used as part of a trigger for an atom bomb,' Glover replies, with a lifetime of accumulated wisdom, 'That remains to be seen . . .' Caine calls him a complete arsehole and is promptly suspended for insubordination. Come to think of it, the name John Preston is obviously an alias; perhaps he really is Harry Palmer after all.

The Whistle Blower (1986) was Caine's first project after his move back to England, where he had bought a house in Oxfordshire. Though life as a Beverly Hills tax exile had suited the sybaritic side of his nature, he had always been an Englishman at heart. He missed the English weather, and he missed Harrods. 'There are swings and roundabouts,' he joked about living in America. 'You wind up in a classless society with a lot of people who don't have any class.'

He was finally forced to acknowledge his homesickness when his wife caught him re-running videotapes of *Black Beauty,* not for the horses but for the glimpses of English countryside in the background. And he and Shakira decided it would be better for Natasha to be educated at an English school rather than a Californian one. But Caine's years in the United States had been important for his career. He had made enough films, and enough good ones, to confirm his reputation as a world-class film star. He might not be on the spot in Hollywood any more, but Hollywood now knew all about him.

Caine did *The Whistle Blower* for less than his usual fee; it was part of his policy of encouraging work by first-time directors. It is a typically British production, dense and drab, with no hint that anyone knew how to structure a narrative or enhance it with an appropriate visual style. Caine plays Frank Jones, a veteran, like the actor himself, of the Korean war. Frank's son Bob (Nigel Havers), a Russian-speaking linguist working at GCHQ in Cheltenham, expresses disillusionment with his job before dying in a mysterious fall from the roof of his house, apparently after being tripped up by a tabby cat. It turns out that Jones Junior, and several of his colleagues, have been deemed expendable by the authorities, who have been allowing the CIA to stamp out suspected security leaks in order to preserve American confidence in British Intelligence and distract attention away from a highly-placed mole.

The Whistle Blower was the feature debut of Simon Langton, who had directed the television adaptation of John Le Carré's *Smiley's People.* The prevailing tone of the story is paranoia, crying out for an expressionistic or *film noir*-ish approach to emphasise the labyrinthine coils of the plot, but all we get is that Great British standard, all-purpose, non-specific TV docudrama look suggestive of *Panorama,* or possibly *Crimewatch UK.* There are too many facts jostling for inclusion in the screenplay, and not enough organisation of the material into a coherent storyline. There are also some cringe-worthy lines of dialogue, such as when a friend of Bob's tells his grieving father, 'Bob was like Dostoevsky's Idiot, no help to anybody.'

And there is a spectacularly clumsy bit of exposition when we see a crusading left-wing journalist driving along the road for a rendezvous to deliver vital information to Frank, while Frank's voice explains in a voice-over – ostensibly to his son's ladyfriend rather than to the audience – 'He couldn't give me the name over the phone in case it was bugged, but we're to meet him at the junction of the A4 and the A7.' One's heart immediately plummets, not because we are fearful about what will happen to the crusading, left-wing journalist, but because what will happen to him is all too drearily obvious. And yes, here's a big lorry, and oh dear he's trying to overtake it, and *boom*! Goodbye, crusading left-wing journalist.

Once again it is Caine's performance which virtually binds the whole film together. Frank Jones is not your average hero, but he changes as the story progresses, from a patriot with an unquestioning faith in authority into a solitary ex-soldier determined not to give in to the institutionalised paranoia that has corrupted every-

Caine playing a father with a grown-up son; with Nigel Havers in **The Whistle Blower**

thing he once thought was worth fighting for. He is a sentimental man, but stubborn, and he will stick to his guns for what he thinks is right. As he sticks to them, he grows in stature from a soldier ant to a hero. 'I'll tell you what I want,' he says near the end of the film, 'I want to believe in England again,' and for once, such a line doesn't sound hackneyed.

In scene after scene, Caine strips the art of screen acting down to its minimal components. When he is informed of his son's death, for example, there is barely a flicker of reaction on his face, and yet we can tell he is devastated. One of his most fascinating scenes is the Fake Drunk Scene, when he is pretending to get sozzled in the company of Barry Foster, an old friend who he knows was instrumental in setting up Bob's murder. Lurching around one minute, quickly spiking the tonic water with vodka the next, the boozy amiability gradually gives way to implacable relentlessness as he senses Foster is leading up to a confession.

29

DISASTER REVISITED

Jaws – The Revenge (1987), which might as well have been called *Jaws 4,* makes *Jaws 2* and *Jaws-3-D* look like masterpieces. (One hesitates to mention the original Steven Spielberg *Jaws* in the same breath.) This clumsy, inept sequel starts off with a great white shark snacking on one of the sons of the late Police Chief Brody. Brody's widow becomes convinced that the shark is deliberately stalking members of her family, hence the movie's catchy ad-line – 'This time it's *personal*'. So what does she do? She moves to the Bahamas, where there's *lots* of water to get nervous about.

Also in the Bahamas is Michael Caine as Hoagie, the local expatriate pilot ('I'm a pilot; my vision is perfect') and gambler who takes a fancy to Mrs Brody and shows her a good time in the local bars. Meanwhile, her worst fears are confirmed – the great white has followed her all the way from Amity Island and is now eyeing up her surviving son, a marine biologist and snail expert, with a view to adding him to its dinner menu. Mrs Brody's small granddaughter has a close call when the shark sneaks up on some children, though the only person who gets eaten is an unnamed adult extra.

In a less than breathtaking showdown, Mrs Brody, her son Michael, Michael's friend Jake and Hoagie all go after the shark, which turns out to be a pretty lame excuse for a man-eater, since it fails dismally in its attempts to eat Hoagie's seaplane with Hoagie inside it, and demonstrates further signs of rubber-monster myopia by overlooking Jake when he tries to hurl himself down its throat. Mrs Brody, armed with little more than one or two inspiring flashbacks of her late husband, finally puts the beast out of its misery by ramming it to death with her boat.

It should perhaps be pointed out that Mrs Brody, by far the least interesting character in the original *Jaws,* is played by Lorraine Gary, who just happens to be married to Sidney Sheinberg, head of Universal, which owns the *Jaws* franchise; she is not a bad actress, but one doesn't exactly ferment with curiosity as to whether or not the shark will eat her. Never mind exciting story, interesting characters, artistic quality, awe-inspiring special effects – all elements in which this film is spectacularly lacking. If there's one thing a killer-shark film can't do without, it's a body-count. In *Jaws – The Revenge,* the final score is Humans 1: Sharks 2, which is pathetic; with a hundred minutes of running-time, that makes it only one casualty every half-hour, which leaves an awful lot of yawn-making longueur in between. The film was apparently re-edited after its original American release so that more of the characters survived; if the film-makers had had any sense at all, they should have re-edited it so that *no one* was left alive.

Caine said he took the role for four reasons: 1) the Bahamas location; 2) the money; 3) his fourteen-year-old daughter persuading him to make a film which her friends would want to see; and 4) the script. The first three reasons, at least, are understandable. Another reason which surfaced at a later date, though it didn't sit quite so well with the flippant persona he liked to present to the press, was that it was economically necessary to accept roles in big-budget films such as *Jaws – The Revenge* if he wanted to appear in low-budget projects such as *The Whistle Blower,* a first film by an unknown director.

30

THE COCKNEY CARY GRANT

For *Surrender* (1987), Caine was reunited with Sally Field, the world-class specialist in chirpiness with whom he had shared the screen in *Beyond the Poseidon Adventure.* Caine plays Sean Stein, a successful novelist whose unfortunate experiences with women (his wife sues him for alimony, his girlfriend for palimony, and a hooker locks him in the bathroom and steals his car) make him determined to avoid contact with members of the opposite sex. He even considers selling up and moving to Kuwait ('cos women can't vote and they flog them'). Nowadays, of course, Kuwait doesn't seem such an attractive proposition, even for a confirmed misogynist.

All his intentions fly out of the window, however, when a gang of robbers disrupts the party he is attending and forces the guests to take their clothes off. Caine finds himself tied in an extremely compromising position to production-line artist Sally Field. The two fall in love, but Caine, mindful of his past experiences and wanting to be loved for himself rather than for his money, pretends to be a struggling unpublished writer. After numerous misunderstandings and arguments on pre-nuptial agreements, a trip to Las Vegas where Field wins a fortune on the slot machines, and several close calls with Field's mercenary ex-boyfriend (Steve Guttenberg), the couple end up as they met, bound naked to each other (by a sympathetic transvestite hooker) and looking set to get married and live happily ever after.

Surrender is a mild romantic romp which, despite the characters' readiness to hop into bed on their first date, has a curiously old-fashioned feel to it. 'I've always wanted to be in a real American screwball romantic comedy like they used to make before the war,' said Caine, who rather liked being referred to as the Cockney Cary Grant. He had almost played the Cary Grant role in *Switching Channels,* an updated remake of *His Girl Friday* with Kathleen Turner as a star TV reporter. But problems with the mechanical shark on *Jaws – The Revenge* had kept him in the Bahamas, the role went to Burt Reynolds instead, and the film flopped like a wet fish.

Caine with pipe and deerstalker in **Without a Clue**

Caine dutifully predicted *Surrender* would be his biggest box-office hit to date. Alas, though Jerry Belson's screenplay was better than his direction, *Surrender* ended up a dull, rather plodding affair with none of the zip or wit of the great screwball comedies, and it failed to make an impact on either critics or audiences. From the very beginning, it boded ill that the production company was Cannon, not exactly known either for its light touch or the magic touch at the box-office. Film buffs, incidentally, may be able to spot a bit of in-house plugging, or perhaps it's in-house cost-cutting; Caine and Field go to see the film of Verdi's *Otello* – which also happened to be produced by Cannon – and at another point Field's television gives us a blast of the soap opera *Dynasty* – produced by Aaron Spelling, who *just happened* to be producer on *Surrender* as well. Cheaper than having to shell out for someone else's extracts.

There can be few complaints, however, about the film's stars, even if (at 54 and 41 respectively) they are both pushing the outside of the envelope as conventional romantic leads. They ping-pong lines off each other as if they were dealing with the wittiest dialogue since Noël Coward, Oscar Wilde and *Bringing Up Baby* rolled into one. The fact that neither of them is in the final flush of youth (and that Caine, at least, does not have the appearance of one-who-works-out-at-the-gym) makes their love scenes rather touching. If you can't actually work up much concern for the characters, the actors themselves are still very likeable, and Caine's dry approach has rubbed off some of Field's excess sugar content. For hardcore Caine fans, there is the added bonus of a rather good Drunk Scene.

Caine's ability to play a light romantic lead in his fifties is a trait he shares with Cary Grant. He is one of those actors whose sexuality has not diminished but deepened through the years. 'It's something about the eyes – blue, penetrating, always slightly amused,' Jackie Collins wrote in *Interview* magazine. 'He's also very wise, witty and smart: a lethal combination.'

It is part of Caine's professionalism – not to mention loyalty to his wife – that there has never been any hint of romantic involvement with a single one of his co-stars over the years. Caine's belief is that such emotional entanglements would weaken his performance. Certainly there would be complications if a close relationship were to split up in the middle of a production, as happened with Al Pacino and Diane Keaton during the filming of *Godfather III*. Caine is friendly towards his leading ladies, and he jokes with them to ease the tension in love scenes, but nothing more.

One of the biggest – and least acknowledged – problems with comedy is that, if something goes wrong, the result is just not funny, whereas serious films, when botched, are often full of unintentionally comic moments. *Without a Clue* is a one-joke movie, and even the one-joke isn't terribly amusing. The film is amiable enough in a rambling, inconsequential kind of way, providing one doesn't pay it too much attention.

Michael Caine gets to don the famous Sherlock Holmes deer-stalker, although he isn't actually playing Sherlock Holmes – the twist being that Holmes is really a figment of Dr Watson's imagination. Watson has hired a dimwitted actor called Reginald Kincaid to pose as the fictional detective he has created as a front for his own powers of deduction, though he is continually exasperated by the way in which Holmes is hailed as a Great Detective while he himself is dismissed as a buffoon.

The main problem with this is that in every Conan Doyle story, in every film and television adaptation, in every interpretation of Sherlock Holmes from Clive Brook and Basil Rathbone to Peter Cushing and Jeremy Brett, the most intriguing, fascinating and entertaining aspect of the story has always been the character of Sherlock Holmes himself. No matter that the mysteries revel in exotic and sinister titles, nor that they are replete with brain-boggling clues; they are merely a means to an end, namely as an excuse to put the great man through his paces, demonstrating his eccentricity as well as his intellect, allowing him to play the violin, sniff cocaine and puff on his pipe. Take away the character of Holmes, or replace him with an impostor, and what have you got? Not a lot. Not even Michael Caine can rescue a story so hell-bent on self-destruction as to do away with the very character who has always been its mainstay.

You have, of course, still got Dr Watson – and admittedly he did strike out on his own in *The Hound of the Baskervilles*. But even this Watson has undergone a major transformation, as played by Ben Kingsley, into a cunning, rather vain individual, not the Watson we know and love at all.

Conan Doyle this most definitely is not, and even the baddies – Professor Moriarty and his cohorts are planning to cripple the economy by flooding it with forged five pound notes – come across as rather half-baked in their villainy. Watson disappears during a fight on the docks, Kincaid is forced to draw on real powers of detection in order to trace him, and the bad guys are arrested or dispatched. In the end, the pseudo-Holmes and the real Dr Watson are left with a genuine buddy-buddy relationship.

Compared with the exemplary Granada TV series starring Jeremy Brett, *Without A Clue*'s production values look pretty hokey,

very much the American idea of Victorian England, all horses clip-clopping over cobbled streets, shiny steam engines chuff-chuffing up antique branch lines, and loveable urchins with stage-school accents. Caine, an intelligent man impersonating a stupid man who is impersonating an intelligent man, delivers his customary Drunk Scene with panache, but never really convinces as someone who would pass as the Great Detective; it might have been amusing to see him playing it straight. He is replaced by a stunt double in some convoluted slapstick, but gets to do his own fencing at the climax, which takes place in a gaslit theatre.

Sherlock Holmes can stand some larking about, but this looks tame when compared to the boisterous farce of Paul Morrissey's *Hound of the Baskervilles,* let alone when set up against Billy Wilder's inspired and melancholy *The Private Life of Sherlock Holmes.* Nor is it even as exciting as the Spielberg-produced *Young Sherlock Holmes and the Pyramid of Fear;* it is as though the screenwriters, having had their idea, have sat back expecting the professionalism of the performers to do the rest.

And professionalism they have, in spades. Ben Kingsley, talking to Brian Case in *Time Out,* offered an illuminating insight into Caine's methods. 'We work in very similar ways. Our Winnebagos are parked together, you can hear me pacing up and down doing my lines by myself, and he's doing exactly the same thing in his. Pacing up and down, working on rhythms, timings, inflections, working on his voice like a theatre actor.'

Dirty Rotten Scoundrels (1988) was a remake of *Bedtime Story* (1964), starring Marlon Brando and David Niven as two rival conmen competing for the attentions of the same woman. Did Maurice Micklewhite ever have an inkling that he would one day be taking on a role originally played by Niven, Hollywood's most urbane Englishman? Caine is perfect as Lawrence Jamieson, an urbane conman who works the French Riviera town of Beaumont-sur-Mer, divesting gullible women of their riches by pretending to be an exiled prince fighting to save his country from Communism. Jamieson has even got the local police-chief (played by Anton Rodgers, who last appeared with Caine as the weak-kneed traitor in *The Fourth Protocol*) in his pocket, and lives in some luxury in a splendid mansion overlooking the Mediterranean.

One day his comfortable way of life is threatened by Freddy Benson, a brash American newcomer who tries to muscle in on his territory. Benson refuses to be discouraged by Jamieson's attempts to get rid of him, even when he is thrown in jail. In the end, Jamie-

Sherlock Caine and Ben Kingsley investigate **Without A Clue**

son is forced to take him on board as a trainee, schooling him in the finer points of etiquette and allowing him to participate in his scams by pretending to be his lunatic younger brother, Prince Ruprecht. But Benson rebels, and Jamieson devises a contest; whichever of them is first to extract fifty thousand dollars from newly arrived soap queen, Janet Colgate, wins the exclusive right to operate in the town, while the loser will have to quit the Riviera.

Caine shows Steve Martin how it should be done in **Dirty Rotten Scoundrels**

In the ensuing battle of wits, Benson wins Janet's sympathy by pretending to be a crippled naval officer. Jamieson strikes back by popping up as Dr Emil Schauffhausen from Lichenstein, whose miracle treatment of the 'cripple' includes whacking him on the knees with a cane. Finally, in a somewhat predictable but pleasurable twist, the men discover that Janet has been conning them all along and has run off with a bagful of their money.

Dirty Rotten Scoundrels is a breeze of a movie, as enduring as the bubbles in a glass of champagne – the sort of film which is harder than it looks to get right. It is set in a never-never land where it is always sunny, where crimes are committed but no-one ever seems to be a victim of them. It is also fascinating to see the contrast in acting styles of Michael Caine and Steve Martin. Martin, as always, is a superb comic athlete, contorting his body and doing a wide variety of silly walks. It takes someone of Caine's calibre to steal the show, simply by refusing to play for obvious laughs and approaching a comic role as he would a straight one. He even manages to underplay it when speaking with a cod German accent as Dr Schauffhausen. 'Tell me if you feel zis,' he says, grasping the foot which Steve Martin insists is paralysed. 'Tiggle, tiggle, tiggle.'

Caine's performance reinforces one's suspicions that he is one of the best actors in films; his touch is sure, his timing terrific. He is utterly convincing as the man about town who likes to live the good life and who finances it by pretending to be other people; in other words, not a million miles away from the man himself. Niven or no Niven, though it was *Surrender* which was supposed to have given him a Cary Grant-type role, it was *Dirty Rotten Scoundrels* which pulled it off.

31

JACK-IN-THE-BOX

Television had changed in the nineteen years since Caine had last appeared in a drama on the box. Back in the Sixties, the difference between films and television was obvious: one was wide-screen, with lots of colour, big stars and expensive effects, the other was small and usually monochrome. By the end of the Eighties, however, the lines had blurred. All the big film studios now had fingers in the television pie; the Twentieth Century Fox logo, for example, can be seen after each episode of the TV series *LA Law*. At times, the British film industry seems to have consisted of nothing but films financed by Channel 4. In all the film-making countries of the world, video, cable and television companies provide backing for films in return for the rights to screen them after their theatrical release.

That peculiar hybrid the 'Made for TV Movie' muddles the issue even further. Occasionally, films made for television in one country will end up in another country on the big screen; the most famous example of this was Steven Spielberg's 1971 film *Duel*, which was made for television but released on to the British cinema circuit. Nowadays, it is not always possible to pick up a video cassette and know whether its content started out in cinemas or on American television. Another development is the mini-series – a story which is chopped into film-length chunks, usually shown on consecutive evenings, full of big-name film-stars, and screened with all the fanfare appropriate to something with a budget often exceeding that of the average film. Michael Caine's return to television was in one such mini-series.

These days, there is no danger of him being mistaken for a television actor. *Jack the Ripper* (1988) was financed by Thames TV and Lorimar, an American entertainment company which insisted the leading role be filled by an international star, and it was in this capacity that Caine reappeared on the small screen. Producer/director David Wickes had previously straddled the television-cinema divide with the spin-off *Sweeney!*, based on the TV series.

Caine plays Inspector Frederick Abberline, the detective who worked on the Ripper case in real life, though of course in real life

the murderer was never caught. The actor was reunited with several blasts from his past: Michael Gothard, who had raped and pillaged in *The Last Valley,* played the anarchist who stirs up the rhubarbing proletariat; Ray McAnally, from *The Fourth Protocol,* played a surgeon; Susan George, from *Billion Dollar Brain* and *The Jigsaw Man,* played a prostitute; Lysette Anthony, from *Without a Clue,* played another prostitute (and they say they don't write parts for women). The series was commissioned to coincide with the hundredth anniversary of the Ripper murders, and Wickes, who had been given access to Scotland Yard's files on the case, had come up with what he reckoned was the definitive solution to the mystery. He shot four different endings, so there would be no chance of the killer's identity being leaked to the press before the series was broadcast; not even the actors knew who it was.

Caine is fine as the detective, battling with a drink problem and revisiting his roots in the East End, but the mini-series is a bit of a plod, not nearly as much fun as more fanciful variations on the case, such as the film *Murder By Decree,* in which Sherlock Holmes investigates the murders. Jane Seymour is there to provide Abberline with romantic interest and point her bustle, but her role seems increasingly irrelevant as the story goes on. The whodunnit aspect of the plot has been elevated over everything else, so that the screenplay has to offer a number of equally plausible suspects. When the man who has been carving up prostitutes, slicing off their ears and eating their kidneys is finally unmasked, Lewis Collins, Caine's sidekick, exclaims in surprise, 'He's mad!' Incidentally it was Ray McAnally what done it.

In *Jack The Ripper,* Armande Assante plays one of the suspects, an actor playing the lead in a stage production of *Dr Jekyll and Mr Hyde.* Perhaps it was this which gave David Wickes the idea for his next collaboration with Michael Caine, a television movie of *Jekyll and Hyde* – the actor's third appearance in a Robert Louis Stevenson adaptation, and a return to the cobbled streets, clip-clopping hooves and gaslights of ersatz Victorian London from *Jack The Ripper* and *Without a Clue.* Caine, who might have been reluctant to follow Fredric March and Spencer Tracy in the dual role on the big screen, relished the challenge of doing it on television. After being away from the box for so long, he was now enjoying his return to it as a leading man. 'The great thing is, they concentrate on the actor,' he said. 'It's your performance they're shooting, and you don't have to wait for the cavalry to come over the hill for an hour before they shoot your close-up.'

Back on the box; Caine as Detective Inspector Abberline in **Jack The Ripper**

No sooner has *Jekyll and Hyde* begun than Caine is demonstrating the two sides of his personality. As Mr Hyde, he knocks a little girl beneath the hooves of a passing horse, giving her a cranial haemorrhage. Changing back into Dr Jekyll, he performs an impromptu brain operation and saves her life. This is already much more fun than *Jack The Ripper,* and when Cheryl Ladd appears with her platinum blonde hair and heaving décolletage, you know you're in for a treat. Not only do we get Hyde behaving very badly towards women, setting fire to pubs and cackling 'Ha ha ha ha ha ha *haaar!*' all over the place, we also get a romantic montage of Jekyll and Cheryl doing all the things that lovers do – playing badminton, posing for photographs, going to the opera, playing peek-a-boo.

The pay-off is at the end, when Jekyll is trying to kill himself and Hyde is trying to stop him so he can carry on with his evil ways, cackling and setting fire to pubs. In a scene which conjures fond memories of his wrestling match with the severed hand in *The Hand,* Caine struggles with himself for control of the revolver. As Jekyll, he shouts, 'Yes! Yes' and points the gun at his head. As Hyde, he shouts 'No! No!' and thrusts it away. Then, as Jekyll he shouts 'Yes! Yes!' again. And so on, until the best man wins.

'I've been told I have a Victorian face,' Caine said. 'Mind you, I dislike the stiff collars, the fog and gloom, and cobwebs getting up your nose – although I enjoyed smashing up the lab.' Ever since James Clavell had given him tips on Japanese equanimity during the filming of *The Last Valley,* he had kept his temper under control. Now he enjoyed the opportunity to bang on tables and throw people through windows. 'I loved every second of it,' he said.

He had worn heavy make-up for *Sleuth,* but it was as nothing compared to what he had to put up with in *Jekyll and Hyde.* The prosthetic make-up for Mr Hyde took four hours to apply, and then he wasn't allowed to eat anything greasy in case it stained the latex. There was a not entirely unwelcome side-effect; after five weeks of lettuce and radishes, the actor found he had lost half a stone. 'Thanks for the diet, guys,' he said.

Michael Caine has made two other notable television appearances in recent years. In 1987, he conducted a BBC master class on film acting. Not only was this informative and entertaining, packed with anecdotes from his career, it also gave some indication of the dedication with which Caine approaches his job – the hard work which he usually makes light of. This wasn't a tutorial on how to get to the heart of the character you're playing, it was a nuts-and-bolts exposé of the things a screen actor *really* needs to know, such as which eye to look through, or where to stand, or what to do when your co-star tries to upstage you.

In Caine's terms, preparation for a role doesn't mean learning to speak Polish in order to play a concentration camp inmate, or confining yourself to a wheelchair for several weeks in order to play a paraplegic, or spending four days locked up in San Quentin in order to play a convict – all those nutty, lovable things which American Method actors get up to. Caine's idea of preparation means learning lines, working out movements, trying out the doors on the set to make sure they don't stick. He takes the mystique out of it – which results, paradoxically, in making screen acting look *even harder* than it looked to begin with. That one-off perfect film performance which we think we all have up our sleeve – much as we all have a novel in us somewhere – starts to look remote. Clearly, screen acting is no job for amateurs. To work at it for a lifetime requires years of hard grind, total dedication and a constant flow of inspiration.

No wonder Caine was so good as Dr Frank Bryant in *Educating Rita* – he is a natural teacher.

In 1989, London Weekend Television broadcast an hour-long documentary called *The Trouble With Michael Caine,* in which colleagues and acquaintances from all stages of his long career gathered to pay tribute and relate anecdotes. Caine has always refused to appear on *This Is Your Life,* but this was the next best thing. The programme, which was chaired by Michael Aspel, later provided the basis for an entertaining book, *Candidly Caine.*

Caine with his old pal Roger Moore in the slapstick comedy **Bullseye!**

THE NINETIES

Caine cantered into the Nineties with a spirited double attack which demonstrated the two different sides to his approach to the film business. 'When you have a very high standard of living,' he said, 'sometimes you must make a very low standard of movie.' And in the eyes of the critics, he couldn't have got much lower than *Bullseye!*, a slapstick comedy directed by Michael Winner, the film director the critics love to hate. Caine and his old friend, Roger Moore, each play two roles. As Dr Daniel Hicklar and Sir John Bavistock, they make a scientific discovery which will lead to cheap electricity. As their lookalikes, cheap conmen Sidney Lipton and Gerald Bradley-Smith, they get embroiled in the scientists' scheme to sell off their invention to the highest bidder. The trail leads from London, still swinging after all these years, to Scotland, where Caine and Moore dutifully get togged up in kilts and undergo various slapstick humiliations and *Doppelgänger* confusions before heading for the Caribbean with a haul of stolen diamonds. Sally Kirkland provides the clingy skirt interest, and there is a last-minute cameo from John Cleese.

Bullseye! is everything the critics said about it, and worse. The only thing they forgot to say is that it is actually rather enjoyable. It is like a compendium of a half-century of rotten British humour; there are jokes about randy Rottweilers, window-cleaners, Swiss cheese, massage parlours, the Queen's corgis and lots of funny foreigner clichés. England consists of stately homes and quaint villages; Scotland is full of exploding haggises, caber-tossers and Michael Caine, in a kilt, getting a Tug o' War rope caught between his legs. Pandering to the worst common denominator, yes, but irresistible; sometimes, one's worst common denominators need to be pandered to.

A Shock to the System, on the other hand, is a modest film full of interesting but non-commercial quirks, which is lifted quite a few notches by Caine's performance in it. 'I'd been reading lots of scripts, one after the other, and suddenly I read this one,' he said. 'I said "Wait a minute". It's a very funny nightmare, quite frightening, but extremely funny.'

He plays Graham Marshall, an advertising executive whose life is turned upside-down when he is passed over for promotion. 'He's victimised and he knows it,' said Caine. 'I've played a lot of sympathetic villains, and Graham's certainly one of them. All psychotics – and Graham becomes one – are paranoid. They think of themselves as victims. And the reason they kill somebody is because they perceive that somebody to have done them a wrong.'

The accidental death of a tramp under the wheels of a tube train convinces him he can get away with murder, so he sets about removing all the people he believes have wronged him, who also happen to be the obstacles between him and perfect happiness. His wife dies in an 'accident' with the electrical wiring; the arrogant yuppie who stole his promotion dies in an 'accidental' explosion aboard his boat.

The police lieutenant investigating the case (Will Patton, doing a marvellous Columbo impersonation) suspects Graham, but can't prove a thing. Graham's mistress (played by the charming, talented and all too often underused Elizabeth McGovern) discovers the truth about him, but he out-psyches her, and has her safely transferred to another office. The film was originally to have ended with Caine getting his come-uppance, but now it ends, rather daringly, with the idea that he has not only got away with two murders (three counting the other passenger on the boat), but thinks nothing of committing another. Caine's snake-eyed charm in the central role gives the story another, not entirely comfortable twist; we are so completely in sympathy with him that we are quite happy to see some of the other characters die so that he can get what he wants.

Caine supplements the narrative with another of his voice-overs, this one in the third person, talking about himself as if he were a magician or a god. As the film progresses and it looks as though no-one can touch him, he gives a subtle portrayal of a man becoming drunk with his own power, though not so obviously that his colleagues will notice; it is, of course, quite likely that the world of big business is full of people like this, even if they haven't gone quite as far as murder in the ruthless pursuit of their aims. His rage when he learns he hasn't got the job he'd been promised is so intense and frightening that it tips the film from a lightweight black comedy into another dimension altogether, something much more disturbing and psychotic. The film might not be playing for keeps, but its leading actor certainly is.

Growing older has never held any terror for Michael Caine. 'All it means is that I'll probably get more interesting parts.' For most of his career he has declared an interest in the writing and directing side of film-making, though the total, long-term commitment to a project which that would entail has seemed to put him off. He looks on acting as a job which he can leave behind him at the end of the day; writing and directing would require an emotional investment going way beyond that.

'One day I'll be gone,' he said, in rather a fatalistic mood, to John Kobal in *Films and Filming*. 'What I've done is made a good living for myself and my family, and I've had a wonderful time. And that's about all I expect out of it.'

Michael Caine has what all real movie-stars require in order to seize the public imagination – an image so distinctive that he has become a household name, almost an institution. His *Spitting Image* puppet is instantly recognisable to television viewers. His voice and manner are so distinctive that Peter Sellers once impersonated him for the message on his telephone answering machine, and it was Sellers who gave him his own catch phrase – 'Not many people know that' – stemming from Caine's reputation as a voracious reader and fund of useless information.

He has joined the select ranks of actors who have had pop songs dedicated to them (others include Humphrey Bogart in *2HB* by Roxy Music and *Robert De Niro's Waiting* by Bananarama); the London group Madness recorded a song called *Michael Caine* in which Caine's voice can be heard repeating the line 'My name is

Michael Caine'. He has played the publicity game with skill and candour; he has been equally at home talking technique to *Films and Filming* and *Stills*, or dishing the titbits to the tabloids. He has always been a favourite of the popular press, though he never provides them with the sort of hot copy on which they thrive. Both in his public and his private life, he is determinedly non-sensational; Michael Caine is famed for his professionalism, for his affability, and for his rock-solid marriage to Shakira.

Talking about himself and his friends Sean Connery and Roger Moore, Caine has said, 'We are throwbacks to the American actors in the contract studio system, because those were the people we grew up with and admired.' And like the enduring movie stars of the Hollywood studio era, he stamps every performance with his own distinctive image, even though he may be playing a character very different from himself.

But unlike many of the Hollywood greats, Caine has combined his movie-star qualities with the sort of skills traditionally more often expected of supporting players than of stars; he describes himself as a 'Leading Character Actor'. He has no personal vanity, and no qualms about appearing unsympathetic or unattractive. He can carry a film single-handed, or he can blend seamlessly into an acting ensemble. He has emerged with his reputation unscathed, even enhanced, from any number of bad films – and though some are not nearly so bad as some critics would have you believe, others deserve every brickbat they get.

Indeed, Caine's apparent lack of selectivity in choosing his roles is one of the keys to his success; the bad films have not only sustained his career in between the triumphs, they have also provided him with the means of fine-tuning his skills. And the public admires his readiness to take almost any role which comes his way; that he has made so many bad films has, if anything, increased the affection in which he is held. Caine's trick, when reminded of the number of flops he has made, is to point to the career of someone like Clark Gable, who made nearly seventy films – and you would be hard-pressed to find anyone who could name more than ten. If we're considering posterity, then Caine could hold his end up with the best of them: *Zulu, The Ipcress File, Billion Dollar Brain, Alfie, Get Carter, Pulp, The Man Who Would Be King, Educating Rita, Hannah and Her Sisters, Dirty Rotten Scoundrels,* to name but ten, will all be remembered – some, indeed, are already a quarter of a century old and still *are* remembered.

But it is in the shape of rich-and-famous-film-star Michael Caine that Maurice Micklewhite from Rotherhithe has delivered – and is

Mr and Mrs Caine

still delivering – the ultimate in life-long performances; that of a self-made man who has become in reality everything he always dreamed of being. He is living proof that it can be done, that you can come from absolutely nowhere and go absolutely anywhere you want. And he has done it on his own terms, without compromising his integrity or polishing up his vowel sounds, and with a refreshing lack of artistic pomposity and celebrity neurosis. Acting, he said, was 'just something which I kept plugging away at, and tried to do better and better, and tried to get my wages put up, which everybody who works does.'

He's selling himself short; and he knows it, but that's part of the game he likes to play, talking of films as though it were a matter of technique and nothing more. But above and beyond his hard-working professionalism, there is also the secret ingredient. Either the camera loves you, or it doesn't. Michael Caine is not your average good-looking jock with a tan and endless cheekbones, but the camera loves him like mad. At an American Film Institute tribute to John Huston, there were film clips of Bogart in *The Maltese*

Falcon, Bogart and Hepburn in *The African Queen,* Gable and Monroe in *The Misfits.* The last clip was of Caine and Connery in *The Man Who Would Be King.* Neither actor seemed out of place in that line-up. 'The hair went up on the back of my neck,' Caine said afterwards.

Michael Caine is one of the world's leading movie-stars. That he has become what he set out to be is a remarkable achievement at the best of times, but even more so since he has spent more time based in Britain than in America, and this in an era when the British film industry has been in a state of terminal decline, and British film-stars are the rarest of breeds, even rarer than British films. 'I'm not an actor who works in the cinema, television, on the stage, a bit of radio,' Caine said in 1971. 'I'm a complete and total cinema man.' He has worked for some of the world's best-known film directors, and appeared opposite some of the world's best-known actors and actresses.

He is the best, most important, and most versatile film-star that Britain has ever produced.

Not many people know that, but it's about time they did.

INDEX

NOTE

Michael Caine's films are listed in the entry for Michael Caine. Page references in italic indicate illustrations.